PAINTING ON GLASS

CONTEMPORARY DESIGNS

—

SIMPLE TECHNIQUES

Paige Gilchrist

LARK BOOKS

A Division of Sterling Co., Inc
New York

ART DIRECTOR: Kathleen Holmes

PHOTOGRAPHY: Sandra Stambaugh

ILLUSTRATIONS: Orrin Lundren

ASSISTANT EDITOR: Catharine Sutherland

EDITORIAL ASSISTANCE: Jamie Ridenhour

PRODUCTION ASSISTANCE: Hannes Charen

Library of Congress Cataloging-in-Publication Data

Gilchrist, Paige
    Painting on glass : contemporary designs, simple techniques / Paige Gilchrist.—1st ed.
        p.   cm.
    Includes index
    ISBN 1-57990-155-7
    1. Glass painting and staining—Patterns.   I. Title.
    TT298.G55 2000
    748.5'028'2—dc21

10 9 8 7 6 5 4 3 2 1

First Edition

Published by Lark Books, a division of
Sterling Publishing Co., Inc.
387 Park Avenue South, New York, N.Y. 10016

© 2000, Lark Books

Distributed in Canada by Sterling Publishing, c/o Canadian Manda Group, One Atlantic Ave., Suite
105, Toronto, Ontario, Canada M6K 3E7

Distributed in Australia by Capricorn Link (Australia) Pty Ltd., P.O Box 6651, Baulkham Hills,
Business Centre NSW 2153, Australia

If you have questions or comments about this book, please contact:
Lark Books
50 College St.
Asheville, NC 28801
(828) 253-0467

Printed in China through Four Colour Imports

ISBN 1-57990-155-7

Contents

Painting on Glass. Are We Kidding?

We hear your questions, loud and clear: *"Glass? And painting? You expect me to combine one of the world's most intimidating raw materials (it's fragile, it breaks into jillions of pieces) with one of art's most daunting techniques (isn't painting reserved for eccentric geniuses who wear only black and do their best work at 2 a.m.?). Then you have the nerve to call it fun—for home crafters?"*

Relax, and forget the formidable ring of the words in the title. (We have much more encouraging ones for you, including "amazing ease, instant gratification, and no painting experience required.") Read on.

You know how the lucky among us have that single dessert recipe that we absolutely love? The one that requires nothing more than a few embarrassingly simple steps, yet results in a gourmet masterpiece that has everyone at the table oohing and ahhhing? This is a book full of the paint-and-glass equivalents of those recipes. Pick it up, pick a project to start on, and in no time you'll be whipping up your own spectacular versions of the bright, bold pieces of painted glassware that have become some of today's hottest home accessories.

Even if you think—before you get started—that working on glass will shatter your nerves. Even if holding a paintbrush feels foreign—at first.

This book's eclectic group of 60 projects, featuring everything from pitchers and bowls to platters, candleholders, cups, and doorknobs, reminds you that few of us go through a day without handling plenty of glass. It's not all delicate crystal. We rely on glass objects to hold toothbrushes, serve iced tea, contain salads as they're being tossed, and bake casseroles. Think of it that way, and you realize how durable most glass is. It's going to survive a bit of artistic attention—and be the better for it.

What's more, if you can follow a line as you dab on color, you can paint any piece in this book. If a project calls for a painted image that is more complicated than a polka dot, we've provided a pattern, along with a selection of simple methods for transferring it to your glass. Once you've done that, simply follow the project instructions. They spell out which paint color goes where and tell you exactly how to apply it. (And, by the way, you don't always have to use a paintbrush. Sponging, stamping, and squeezing paint straight from the bottle are options, too.)

Every project in the book shares a common ingredient: new paints now on the market that are designed especially for easy use on glass. Some shimmer, some simulate stained glass and leading, some will coat your glass objects in bright opaque colors, others are translucent and catch the light. Most air dry quickly; others you simply bake for 30 minutes in a conventional oven to "fix" your design. We give you a primer on what's available and how to use each type of paint. Then, 26 top designers show you how with 60 diverse projects.

We cover all the latest looks for painted plates, drinking glasses, bowls, platters, pitchers, bottles, vases, and more, giving you designs you can use to liven up everything in your kitchen cabinets. When you're ready to move on to the garage, the hardware store, or your favorite flea market (or maybe you'd like to start there?), we offer plenty more projects to guide you. Want to dust off and revive old windows and doors, for example? We show you imaginative ways to transform them into painted glass room dividers, decorative fireplace screens, wall hangings, and more.

Finally, when the inevitable I'll-paint-any-piece-of-glass-I-can-get-my-hands-on spirit takes over, you can choose from designs for everything from water coolers and mirrors to garden lights, clocks, tea lanterns, jewelry, and tabletops.

At some point early on in this process, you'll realize we aren't kidding at all when we pair the words painting and glass—but we are having quite a bit of fun with the combination. We're pretty sure you will, too.

Glass from the Past: A Brief History

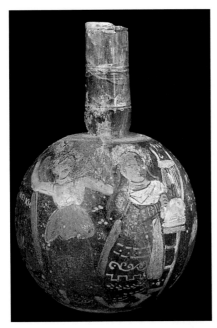

Cold painting and gilding were used to adorn this blown-glass bottle with images of Apollo and Marsysas. An example of Roman empire glass, it was created in the third to fourth century A.D.

Glass has existed on earth for millions of years. For as long as the natural processes of our planet have run their course, molten lava has cooled and formed obsidian, electrified forks of lightning have transformed grains of sand into fulgurite, and meteorites crashing to earth have produced tektites.

These naturally occurring forms of glass—created when heat fuses a mixture of mineral oxides—occasionally became the tools and weapons of primitive humans. But human efforts to make glass without the help of volcanoes or lightning bolts date back less than six thousand years. One legend has it that Phoenician sailors camping on a beach with a cargo of soda discovered the process. They lit a fire, the story goes, and set soda blocks in the sand nearby as resting spots for their cooking pots. The next morning, they found that the sand and soda had been fused by the fire, creating glass.

Whether the specific account is true or not, sand, or silica, was and is the main ingredient in glass. In the early days, sand, a fire, and a substance such as soda (which lowers the sand's melting point) was all one needed to be a glassmaker. Later, glassmakers learned that adding other substances, such as lime, improved the solidity and durability of the final product.

Mesopotamians were the first to make widespread use of artificial glass, though for thousands of years, it was the privilege of only the very rich. As early as 3500 B.C., they were wrapping the prized substance around stone objects and ceramic beads. A thousand years later, the first all-glass objects—primarily amulets and decorative beads—appeared in the same region. After another thousand years, more difficult-to-make hollow vessels such as cups, bowls, and bottles were fashioned out of glass.

Glassmaking as an industry burgeoned under the Roman empire during the first century B.C., when glassmakers on the Phoenician coast discovered glassblowing. By exhaling short puffs of air through a tube into a blob of molten glass,

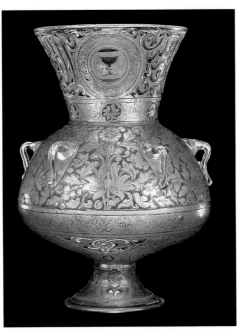

Produced in Syria in the mid-14th century A.D., this blown-glass hanging lamp was decorated with gilding.

glassblowers found, they could quickly inflate forming glass and work it into a great variety of shapes and sizes. The technique revolutionized glass production and transformed glass from a precious commodity into a mass-produced commercial ware.

The beautiful forms and rare colors of Roman glass (which at that time included glass from present-day France, Spain, Portugal, England, Belgium, Switzerland, Turkey, the Middle East, Egypt, North Africa, and parts of the Netherlands, Austria, Germany, and Eastern Europe) led to glass's even greater popularity. From commonplace drinking cups to mold-blown bottles and souvenir beakers (a popular purchase at the chariot races and gladiator contests) to vessels for shipping food and other cargo (an ideal use of glass, as it was transparent, reusable, and did not impart unpleasant flavors), glass was in high demand in Roman society.

American artist William Matthew Prior (1806-1873) reverse painted this portrait of George Washington ca. 1850 using oil on glass.

When the Roman empire fell, glassmaking's popularity plummeted, too. It didn't return to prominence until around 1200 A.D., when French glassmakers settled in Britain and began making glass bottles and other articles. Production of glass for windows began in Britain in 1567, and the industry once again flourished.

From 1400 to 1700, Venice was the center of European glassmaking. There, artisans developed a colorless and transparent glass known as cristallo (because of its resemblance to rock crystal). Their techniques were so prized that the Venetian government sequestered many of its best glassmakers on an island and forbade anyone with knowledge of glassmaking to leave the country. (Punishment for violating the order was death.) Many managed to escape nonetheless—tales of harrowing nighttime getaways abound—and Venetian glassmaking "secrets" spread throughout Europe.

The art of glass painting, which developed during this same time period as a technique for adorning cathedral windows, reached its height in the 16th century. Like glassmaking, glass painting was also shrouded in mystery, though it

A blown-glass beaker from Italy, ca. 1495, featuring Archangel Michael and Saint Catherine. The colorless glass was enameled and gilded.

This glass and sterling silver vase, made by Tiffany and Company ca. 1890, is on display at Biltmore Estate in Asheville, North Carolina.

wasn't government decree that kept knowledge under wraps, but the secrecy of the craftsmen themselves (a much more effective approach, it turns out). Medieval European artists who painted stained glass panels for churches were members of guilds that closely guarded their paint formulas and artistic methods. Few written records were kept, and information about the art form's origins remains sketchy today.

In 1675, an Englishman named George Ravenscroft discovered that the addition of lead oxide to the glassmaking process resulted in a brilliant glass that was much easier to work with and also stronger and heavier. His English lead crystal became the supreme glassware of the 18th century, and it played a key role in the invention of telescopes, microscopes, and other optical lenses.

Mass production of glass didn't begin until 1916, when a papermaker named Irving Colburn invented a way to make glass in large sheets. In 1928, polished plate glass, made by using hand-powered rollers to flatten molten glass, replaced Colburn's sheet glass. Then, in 1959, the "float glass" method was perfected. The process involves floating molten glass on molten tin, where it cools, producing a smooth, even sheet of glass that requires little or no polishing. A high-tech version of the float-glass method is used in industrial glass production today. Computerized systems convert huge amounts of raw ingredients into mass quantities of 4- x 8-foot (1.2 x 2.5 m) sheets of uniformly clear and polished glass.

At the same time that methods for industrial glass production were being refined, modern studio glassmaking was emerging as an art form. Since the early 1960s, glass artists have been exploring the array of possibilities of this versatile substance, which can be blown, cast, ground, fused, etched, sandblasted, spun, mixed with other media, and, of course, painted.

Today, studio glass painters combine glass, a transparent base material available in a tremendous variety of textures and colors, with painting and often firing techniques to enhance its depth and dimension. As the Gallery section beginning on page 114 illustrates, glass painting, which began primarily as a method of architectural decoration, has broadened tremendously in scope, growing into an exquisite form of individual artistic expression.

Basics

The Paints

The current glass-painting craze among crafters can be traced to a single source: new paints!

Basic glass paints made for home craft projects have been around for a couple of decades, but range and availability were limited until recently. Now, versatile, simple-to-use glass paints (which can also be used on everything from ceramics to wood) are filling entire sections of art- and craft-supply shops.

Most are water based, making both setup and cleanup a breeze. Some air dry in minutes. Others you "fire" by baking your painted glass in a conventional oven for half an hour. All now come in a multitude of colors, finishes, and forms.

Following is an overview of what's available.

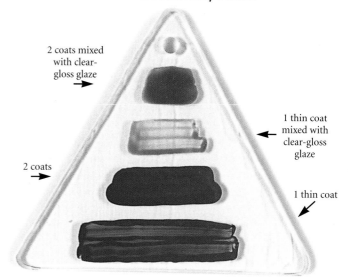

Water-Based Air-Dry Paints

2 coats mixed with clear-gloss glaze →

1 thin coat mixed with clear-gloss glaze ←

← 2 coats

1 thin coat ↙

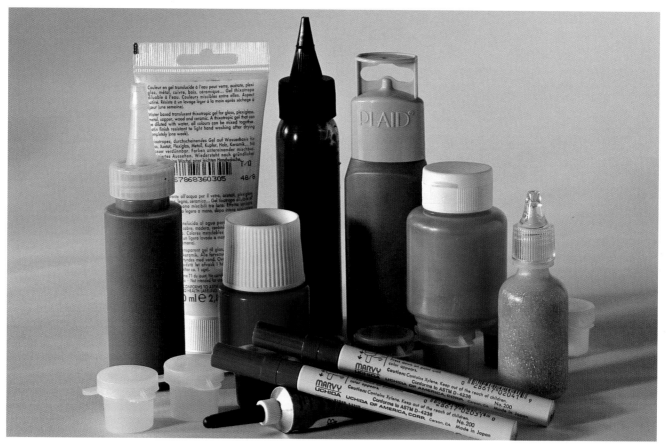

A selection of glass paint

Water-Based Oven-Bake Paints

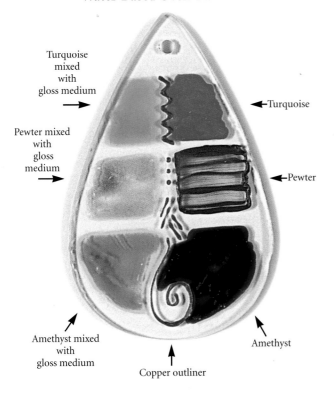

Turquoise mixed with gloss medium →

← Turquoise

Pewter mixed with gloss medium →

← Pewter

Amethyst mixed with gloss medium ↗

Amethyst

Copper outliner

Water-Based Gel Paints

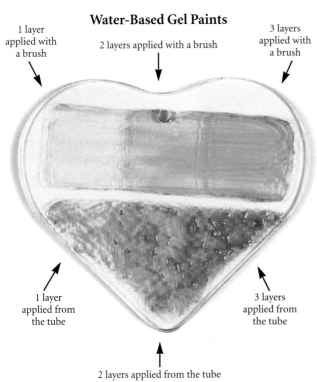

1 layer applied with a brush

2 layers applied with a brush

3 layers applied with a brush

1 layer applied from the tube

3 layers applied from the tube

2 layers applied from the tube

Water-Based Glass Paints

Easy is the watchword here. You can dip your brush right into a bottle of water-based glass paint. Others you can use straight out of a tube or even a spray can. There's no measuring or custom mixing required (a quick stir or shake gets your paint ready to go), and water is all you need to clean brushes when you switch colors. They lend themselves beautifully to layering and blending. And they're also forgiving; you can quick-fix mistakes with a moistened cotton swab.

Under the broad heading of water-based glass paints, there are two different types.

↞ No-bake paints air dry. All you do is paint them on and let your painted piece sit for a couple of days. Since they're the least durable of all glass paints, they're best suited for decorative items that won't require washing.

↞ Thermohardening paints, once dry, are baked in an oven set at about 300ºF (150ºC) for approximately 30 minutes. Because of this "firing" process, they typically wear better than no-bake paints.

Some water-based glass paints are transparent or translucent; others are opaque. Still others dry with a textured finish, simulating the look of custom stained glass or crackle glass. To make any of them more transparent without thinning the consistency, use a colorless acrylic medium.

Solvent-Based Glass Paints

A tiny bit more trouble, these flammable paints require a well-ventilated room for working and mineral spirits for cleaning up. They're primarily transparent and typically no more durable than water-based paints.

Water-Based Gel Paint for Glass

Squeezed from the tube directly to the glass, these gel paints add three-dimensional color—perfect if you want to embed decorative glass nuggets or beads in your design or simply create a raised effect. You can also shake or stir the gel, and it liquifies so you can brush it on. Glass paint gels are generally translucent when they dry, and their durability equals that of standard no-bake glass paint.

Outliner Paste

If you've ever piped icing onto a Christmas cookie or a cake, you'll be a whiz at using outliner paste. (And if you're not a whiz right away, you'll be pleased to know outliner mistakes can be easily scraped off with a craft knife once they're dry.) Outliner comes in tubes in colors ranging from black to metallic bronze. As the name suggests, it's often used to accentuate the edges of a design. And sometimes it is the design; you can use outliner on its own to pipe dancing figures (see the lamp, page 77), spirals and squiggles (see the ornaments, page 36), and more.

Outliner paste is also occasionally called liquid leading, since it's used to simulate lead in stained-glass-style designs. The name's a bit misleading, though. There's no lead at all in the acrylic paste.

Other Paints

Plenty of designers commandeer other paints for glass painting purposes—with great success. Fabric paints (especially the puffy, glittery types), paint pens (perfect for drawing on intricate dots and doodads), and all-purpose acrylic enamel craft paints can all be used on glass.

The Lowdown

As we said, most glass paints on the market are relatively new. That means they're exciting to experiment with. That also means no one has all the answers about them. Even experienced designers are still mixing and matching paints and techniques to find out what works best. Fortunately, this is play, not work—and the experimenting is part of the fun. Here's how to join in.

1. Sample. Before you commit to one brand's deluxe paint set, purchase a few items here and there, and test them. Learn which paints leave a smooth, opaque finish with a brush and which create a transparent shimmer when sponged on and baked. Practice squeezing

Pens and Glossy Paints

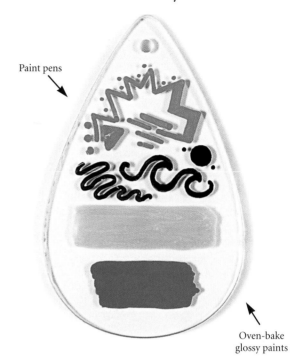

Paint pens

Oven-bake glossy paints

Three-Dimensional Fabric Paints

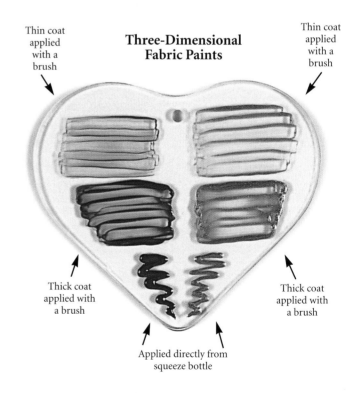

Thin coat applied with a brush

Thin coat applied with a brush

Thick coat applied with a brush

Thick coat applied with a brush

Applied directly from squeeze bottle

Air-Dry Shimmer Paints

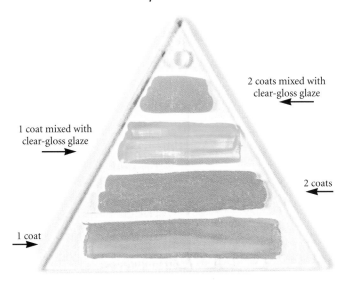

2 coats mixed with clear-gloss glaze

1 coat mixed with clear-gloss glaze

2 coats

1 coat

Crackle Medium and Simulated-Stained-Glass Paint

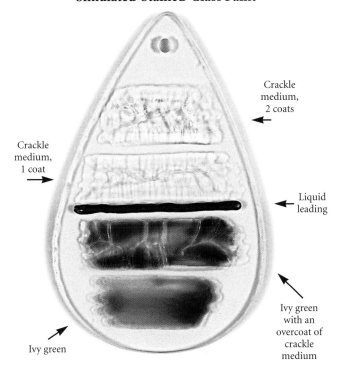

Crackle medium, 2 coats

Crackle medium, 1 coat

Liquid leading

Ivy green with an overcoat of crackle medium

Ivy green

out squiggles from tubes and dabbing on paint with pens. In the end, you may never commit to that deluxe set, but decide you prefer to keep a little bit of a lot of different paints and tools at your fingertips.

2. **Relax.** This will be easier if you're not testing your newly purchased paints on a one-of-a-kind crystal vase. Soak the labels off some bottles in your recycling bin and think of them as free canvases. Then play around (see step 1 above).

3. **Read.** When all else fails (or even before it does), scan the instructions. Manufacturer notes vary on the results you'll get with different paints and processes. Many of the oven-bake paints, they say, are quite durable, even dishwasher safe. Other paints are best used on decorative items you'll be only dusting or, at the most, carefully hand washing. Go ahead and read the directions and disclaimers. (The manufacturers know their products better than anyone; they've also got a bigger stake than anyone in your being pleased with the paint's results.) Then, test what they say on a piece of glass.

Combining Colors

Sometimes, you've got to mix a little peach and persimmon to come up with just the shade of tangerine you're looking for. Custom creating your own colors by blending a few together is easy (not to mention addictive). Here are some simple guidelines.

↪ You'll probably be most successful blending paints that are all the same brand (and, better yet, the same line within that brand).

↪ Don't mix water-based paints with solvent-based paints.

↪ Pick up an artist's color wheel (an inexpensive item available at art and craft supply stores). It'll guide you through the basics of combining blue and red to get purple, and so on.

The Process

Pared down to its major steps, the process for painting on glass really is as easy as one, two, three.

1. Clean and prepare the surface of the glass. Remove any labels or stickers and wash your piece of glass in warm, soapy water, then rinse it thoroughly. After drying the glass completely, wipe the surface with isopropyl alcohol and let it air dry completely before painting on it. Some manufacturers also recommend "conditioning" the glass with their surface conditioner. (Most such conditioners are primarily isopropyl alcohol mixtures).

2. Paint the glass. Of course, this step may involve several stages of its own. We've covered the possibilities in The Techniques, beginning on page 16.

3. Seal your design. Some designers, when working with certain paints, do nothing more than let their painted pieces dry or "cure" thoroughly (usually a few days) to "fix" the design. Others add glaze or gloss as a top coat to seal the work and give the design a more

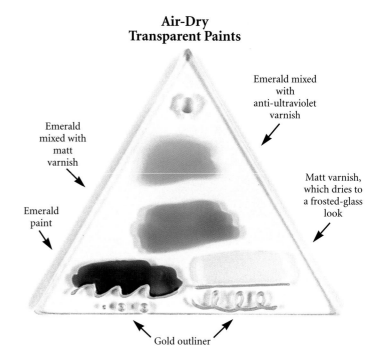

Air-Dry Transparent Paints

Emerald mixed with anti-ultraviolet varnish

Emerald mixed with matt varnish

Matt varnish, which dries to a frosted-glass look

Emerald paint

Gold outliner

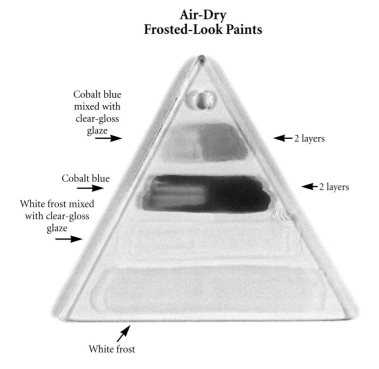

Air-Dry Frosted-Look Paints

Cobalt blue mixed with clear-gloss glaze

2 layers

Cobalt blue

2 layers

White frost mixed with clear-gloss glaze

White frost

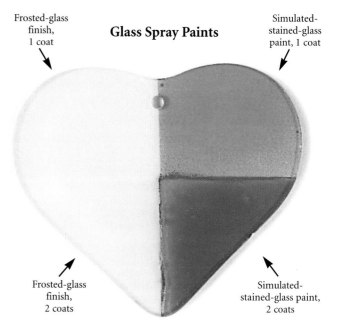

Glass Spray Paints

Frosted-glass finish, 1 coat

Simulated-stained-glass paint, 1 coat

Frosted-glass finish, 2 coats

Simulated-stained-glass paint, 2 coats

Cleaning Old Glass

Glass that's been around for awhile can have lots of character. It can also be cloudy, discolored, or dirty. To clean up clouds and color, try soaking glass pieces in a mixture of one cup (240 mL) of ammonia and four cups (1 L) of warm water. If sediment has adhered to the bottom of a bottle or another piece you want to paint, fill it with white vinegar and water for a few days to soak off the sediment.

polished appearance. (Glazes come in various finishes, from satin to high gloss.) For best results when it comes to adding a top coat, follow the directions on the bottle or tube of paint you're using. If you're working with thermohardening paints, the sealing step involves baking your painted pieces according to the manufacturer's instructions. The baking helps set the paint and smooth out the painted surface.

The Tools & Materials

One quick and inexpensive sweep through the aisles of a craft shop, and you'll have everything you need for most glass-painting projects.

Glass painting tools and materials, clockwise from top right: artist's brushes, mixing palette and palette knife, stencils, stamps, peel-off leading circles, sponges and changeable paint tips, painter's tape, stencil brush and painting sponges, combing tool

13

Artist's Brushes

Stock up on a selection of brushes. They come in a tempting array of shapes (from flat to rounded to fan shaped) and sizes (dainty to substantial). Some are perfect for making delicate dots for flower petals. Others are just the tool for vigorously adding splashy strokes of color.

You'll find brushes labeled with measurements (a ¾-inch [1.9 cm] brush, for example) which tell you the width or diameter of the bristles. Others are numbered (#1 and #6 brushes are common). The lower the number, the finer the line you can paint with it. And some brushes, such as glazing brushes and stippling brushes, have names that tell you what they're best for.

Any glass painter will tell you that brushes are personal business. For the projects that follow, we've noted when a designer recommends a specific type of brush, but feel free to use another one that you like more or that does a better job of creating the look you want.

Stencil Brushes

If you've got to dab paint through the openings of a stencil, these round, stiff-bristled brushes make it easy.

Sponges

Kitchen sponges can be cut into cubes and circles. Cosmetic sponges come in conveniently dainty sizes. Painting sponges can be found on the ends of applicator sticks. And tiny sponges designed specifically for painting are made in shapes ranging from butterflies to fish. All work wonderfully for pressing rather than brushing on your paint.

Palette Knife

This flat plastic tool is handy for spooning supplies of paint out of the bottle and onto a mixing palette, stirring paint, and spreading on thicker gel paints.

Mixing Palette

You can dip your brush straight into the bottles your paint comes in. If, instead, you want the paint more accessible (or plan to mix a couple of colors), shallow plastic lids make fine mini-palettes. But if you respond well to artistic flair (after all, that's half the fun of this), spring for an inexpensive plastic mixing palette. Palettes feature both small slots for individual paint colors and larger areas for blending them together.

Changeable Paint Tips

Changeable tips allow you to alter the look of the line you make when you squeeze paint from a bottle or tube directly to your glass surface. The tips come in both plastic and metal versions, with openings that create everything from large wide lines to tri-line squiggles. Some work only with matching brands of paint, so shop carefully.

Painter's Tape

Painter's tape is designed specifically for masking out straight lines where you want your glass to remain free of paint, as the designer has done on the Fresh as a Daisy project, page 48, for example. Many glass painters find that masking tape or duct tape cut to the desired width works well, too.

Peel-off Leading

Available in strips and circles, ready-to-go pieces of adhesive leading can be peeled off the paper they're packaged on, cut to size (if necessary), and pressed into place on your glass.

Combing Tools

Want wavy stripes or fine-line swirls on your finished surface? Combing tools can be dragged through your wet paint to achieve the effect; see the Cylinder Vase on page 61 for an example. Everyday objects, from toothpicks and knitting needles to erasers, also "etch" interesting patterns into paint. (See page 18.)

Oh Yeah, and the Glass

You know how the minute you add a new term to your vocabulary, you suddenly start hearing and reading it everywhere? You'll experience a similar phenomenon once you turn your attention toward paintable pieces of glass. All of a sudden, you'll notice shelf upon shelf of the stuff, everywhere from home accessory shops and major discount stores to the housewares aisle in the grocery store. You can get glass vases, plates, bowls, and tumblers, of course. But you'll also run across canisters, clocks, light fixtures, and tabletops. Home decorating catalogs stock lots of interesting options. And garage sales and flea markets can be full of one-of-a-kind finds featuring interesting shapes and designs.

Soon after you start noticing all the glass, you'll also begin to see that there are lots of possibilities beyond clear and smooth. Pick up some pieces that are frosted, colored, or cut with a pretty pattern, and play off their added design element when you paint.

Practice Glass

You'll feel freer about testing new paints, experimenting with color combinations, or trying out unfamiliar techniques if you've got some glass around that you're not particularly attached to. Save wine bottles, jelly jars, and other "scrap glass" that you can subject to the early, experimental phases of the creative process.

A collection of glass awaiting paint

The Techniques

Most of the projects in this book call for basic hand painting. Simply select an artist's brush that matches the effect you want to achieve, load it with paint, and begin adding color to your design or brushing on freehand strokes. Some of the projects also incorporate other fun ways to add patterns and pigment to glass.

Sponging

Sponging is one of the most satisfying ways to quickly cover a glass surface with paint. The look can be soft and luminous, you can create different shades by intensifying color in areas where you apply more pressure and contact, or you can achieve a graduated effect by using several colors and blending them into each other. Sponges can also be used for uniform design elements, whether you're dabbing on dots, diamonds, or some other simple shape you've cut from a sponge.

When you're preparing to sponge, think kitchen sponges, sure. Also cosmetic sponges and sea sponges. But keep in mind that you can "sponge" on paint with everything from crumpled newspaper to nubby fabric—all with their own interesting effects.

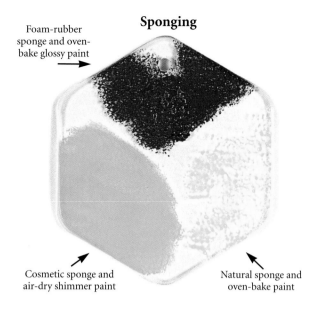

Sponging

Foam-rubber sponge and oven-bake glossy paint →

Cosmetic sponge and air-dry shimmer paint ↗

Natural sponge and oven-bake paint ↖

Stamping

The same kicky stamps that frolic on the front of greeting cards and add panache to handmade paper can be pressed into a pad of permanent ink (or coated with paint) and used to print on glass. And don't stop with the stamps you can buy in craft stores. If paint or ink will adhere to it, you can create a stamp out of it: fruits, vegetables, leaves with pretty patterns, and—most popular—rubber erasers.

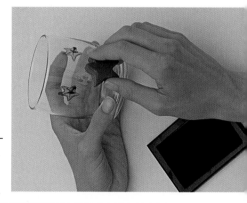

A variety of sponges, including those that come already cut into shapes, can be used to press paint onto glass.

Stamps, whether pressed into an ink pad or coated with paint, are a wonderful tool for "printing" on glass.

Printing

Stenciling   Stamping

Masking

Masking means blocking out areas you want to remain free of paint. You can lay down strips of painter's tape or masking tape, paint over them, pull them up, and be left with crisp, straight lines of clear glass and neat stripes of paint all around them. But beyond tape, you can block the application of paint with any shape you care to cut.

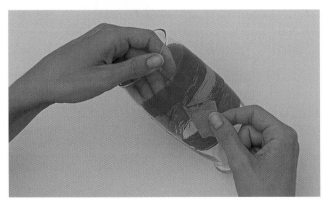

To create crisp, straight lines of unpainted areas of glass, mask off sections with painter's tape or masking tape.

Clip everything from clouds to Christmas trees, use spray adhesive to attach them to your glass, paint all around them, then pull them up.

Stenciling

Stenciling is simply painting through a hole (or pattern of holes) cut in a piece of stencil material that you've taped against the surface of your glass. All you need is a stencil (the pattern of cutout holes), the paint, and a tool for applying the color (paintbrushes, stencil brushes, and sponges are most common). You can purchase stencils at craft stores or make your own. For homemade stencils, choose water-resistant material (such as acetate), and you'll be able to use your stencils over and over.

Stencils provide an easy way to transfer a design to a glass surface.

Outlining

Piping on outliner is easy to get the hang of. Still, you might want to try a few lines and curves on a piece of practice glass or even a sheet of paper first to get a feel for how it works. For a clean, solid line, apply consistent pressure and move the tube along smoothly just above your painting surface. If you press down, you'll stop the flow of outliner and create a gap.

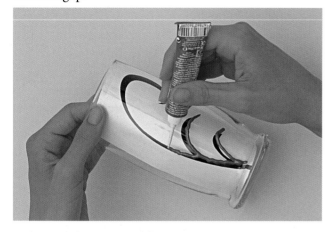

Piping on outliner is a piece of cake—and a lot like decorating one!

Transferring Patterns

You'll want to start many glass-painting projects with a pattern of what you're going to paint already on the glass. Here are three ways to transfer one.

1. Tape the copied pattern to the side of the glass object opposite from the one you'll be painting on (on the inside of a glass, so it shows through on the outside where you'll be painting, for example). Then, simply

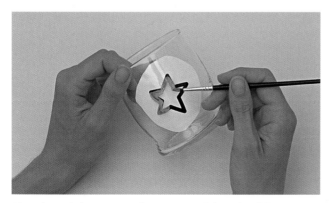

Tape the copied pattern inside your piece of glass, then follow it as you paint.

Brush Techniques

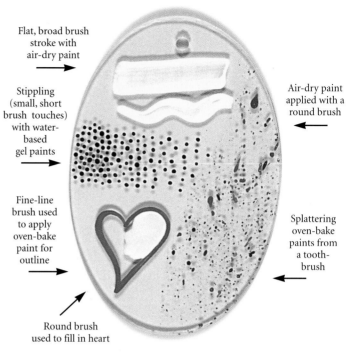

Flat, broad brush stroke with air-dry paint

Stippling (small, short brush touches) with water-based gel paints

Fine-line brush used to apply oven-bake paint for outline

Round brush used to fill in heart

Air-dry paint applied with a round brush

Splattering oven-bake paints from a tooth-brush

Combing

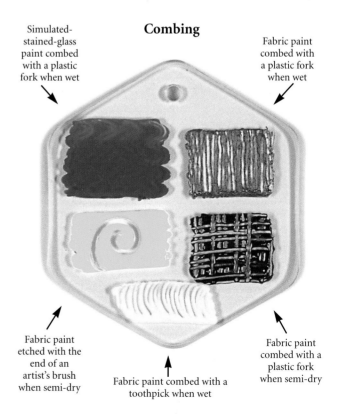

Simulated-stained-glass paint combed with a plastic fork when wet

Fabric paint combed with a plastic fork when wet

Fabric paint etched with the end of an artist's brush when semi-dry

Fabric paint combed with a toothpick when wet

Fabric paint combed with a plastic fork when semi-dry

follow the pattern as you outline and/or paint. If your glass is curved, you may need to cut the pattern into sections and tape them in place separately, working them into the contours of the glass.

2. Cut carefully around the edges of your copied pattern, tape or hold the silhouette to the glass surface on which you'll be painting, trace around it with a water-based marker, then remove the pattern and use the tracing as your guide when you paint.

Trace the pattern on the surface of your piece of glass with a water-based marker.

3. Transfer your pattern to the front of your glass surface with carbon paper. To do this, position the carbon paper on the glass (carbon side against the glass), with the copied pattern on top of it. (Tape the pieces in place if you can. Otherwise, hold them in place with one or more rubber bands.) Draw

over the lines of the pattern with a ballpoint pen. When you remove the pattern and the carbon paper, your design will be outlined on the glass.

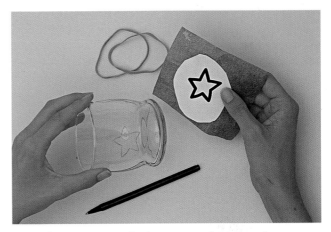

Use carbon paper to transfer the pattern to the surface of your piece of glass.

Touching Up

On the off chance that you're not ecstatic about every stroke you paint, you'll be relieved to know that glass painting is a most forgiving craft. Moisten a cotton swab or paper towel with water or alcohol to wipe off any wet paint that isn't as pleasing (or as perfectly positioned) on the glass as it was in your mind's eye. Once the paint is dry, you can use a craft knife to lightly scrape off bits of paint that have strayed from their intended spot.

Where to Put the Paint

Though some glass paints on the market say they're safe for contact with food and mouths, you may not want your labored-over design to touch either. In that case, always paint on the outside of bowls and plates you'll be using to serve food, and position any paint you're adding to cups or glasses below where people's lips will touch the rim.

Frosted Confetti Bowl

With shimmering splashes of color beaming from the outside in, this mirthful bowl is poised to be the life of any party.

DESIGNER: Tracy Page Stilwell

What You Need

Glass bowl

Glass paints in yellow, Mediterranean blue, turquoise, deep coral, red, white frost, and gold

Outliner (gold)

Painter's tape or masking tape

Medium flat artist's brushes

Hair dryer (optional)

Craft knife

Cosmetic sponge

What You Do

1. Wash and prepare the glass surface.

2. Apply masking tape randomly over the surface of the bowl, leaving spaces of various shapes for paint to adhere. Make sure the edges of the tape are smooth.

3. Working on the outside of the bowl, paint the exposed glass sections in various colors, using one color per section.

4. Once the paint is completely dry, add a layer of white frost paint to each section.

Glass Fact

CUT CRYSTAL GLASS: Created by cutting lead crystal with an iron or stone wheel, cut crystal features groove-like patterns and a brilliant sparkle. The process was developed in the mid-1700s. Hand-cut crystal is still produced today at glassworks such as France's Baccarat and Ireland's Waterford.

5. Let the white layer dry, then add a second coat of your original color to each section. (You can speed up the drying process by applying the heat of a hair dryer to each layer of paint.)

6. Carefully remove the tape. You may have to clean up the edges a bit if paint has seeped under the tape. Use a craft knife to scrape off small errant patches.

7. When you're certain your first layers of paint are dry, add another layer of tape to create another series of exposed sections, and repeat steps 3 through 6.

8. Using the sponge, randomly cover the bowl with gold paint and more white frost paint. Let the paint dry completely.

9. Add accent doodles with gold outliner as the last layer of the piece.

10. Once the paint is thoroughly dry, bake it or glaze it according to the paint manufacturer's directions.

Jazzed-Up Juice Glasses

Unassuming little juice glasses that once blended into the background, upstaged by corn flakes and buttered toast, now spring to life. Breakfast will never be the same.

DESIGNER: Margaret Desmond Dahm

What You Need

Traditional juice glasses with cut bottoms

Glass paints in blue, yellow, and red (or other colors of your choice)

Outliner (black)

Palette or plastic lid for mixing paint

Small artist's brush (no larger than ⅛ inch [3 mm])

Cotton swabs

What You Do

1. Wash and prepare the glass surfaces.

2. Mix a small amount of blue paint with yellow to get a green medium. Add a bit of red to turn the color to amber.

3. Holding a juice glass at the bottom, dab a row of amber dots with the tip of the brush around the top of the glass. Repeat this process on your other glasses.

4. With the full width of the brush, paint a zigzag strip around the middle of each glass. Use the longest cuts in the bottom of the glasses as a rough guide for the top points of the zigzag pattern.

5. Use the black outliner to draw a square spiral set on a diagonal in each "valley" of the zigzag strips. The first two lines of the spiral should mirror the angle of the zigzag's "valley" lines. Slightly damp cotton swabs are the perfect thing for removing any slipups.

6. Once the paint is thoroughly dry, bake it or glaze it according to the paint manufacturer's directions.

Spiral Striped Vase

Make a vase this sharp and sophisticated, and you can start tossing out impressive terms such as "color theory" to all who admire it. (Just between us, all that's involved here is pairing complementary colors, such as the orange on blue in this design. You could also team yellow and purple or green and red for a similar effect.)

DESIGNER: Diana Light

What You Need

> Colored vase (Cobalt blue is featured in this design.)
>
> Glass paints in two shades of a color that complements the vase (such as the two shades of red-orange featured in this design)
>
> Pencil or water-based marker
>
> Artist's brushes (one thinner than the other)

What You Do

1. Wash and prepare the glass surface.

2. Use the pencil or pen to lightly draw two parallel spirals running in a wide fashion down the body of the vase and off its base. If your vase features gentle curves like the one shown in this design, use the curves as a guide, wrapping your spiral pattern around each.

3. Use the thin artist's brush to paint the top spiral in the lighter shade of paint, working from the base of the vase to the top.

4. With the thicker brush, paint the bottom spiral in the darker shade.

5. Once the paint is thoroughly dry, bake it or glaze it according to the paint manufacturer's directions.

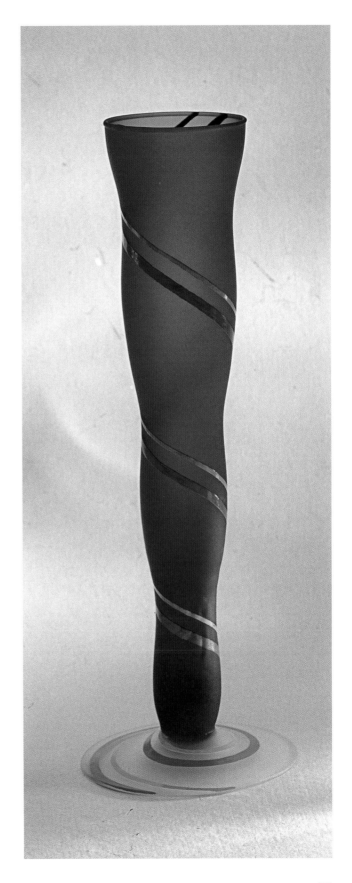

Mardi Gras Martini Set

Splashed with confetti-like spirals and rowdy colors, this boisterous assortment raises spirits even before it's filled with food and drink.

DESIGNER: Katherine Duncan

What You Need

Set of martini glasses

Set of plates

Glass paints in brick red and khaki

Bottle of squeezable glass paint in black

Artist's brush (½ inch [1.3 cm] flat)

What You Do

1. Wash and prepare the glass surfaces.

2. Turn one of the plates face down and, using khaki paint, make radiating marks the width of the brush around the rim, leaving space for adding red and black marks later. (Don't worry about spacing your marks precisely.) Let the paint dry.

3. With a clean, dry brush, add red marks between the khaki ones, leaving slivers of space for adding black lines in the next step. Let the paint dry.

4. Squeeze squiggly black lines and dots onto the remaining unpainted areas around the rim. Let the paint dry.

5. Repeat steps 2 through 4 on the other plates in your set.

6. Place one of the glasses on its rim, and make four khaki marks around the perimeter of the glass, working from the top of the stem up toward the lip, turning the glass by the stem as you paint. (Make sure to leave room between each mark for adding the red marks later.) Let the paint dry.

7. Add a set of red marks between the khaki marks. Let the paint dry.

8. Embellish the glass by squeezing out squiggly black lines and dots over the painted areas. Let the paint dry.

9. Flip the glass over and use a clean, dry brush to paint the base of the glass red. Let the paint dry.

10. Embellish the base with more black squiggles.

11. Repeat steps 6 through 10 on the other glasses in your set.

12. Once the paint is thoroughly dry, bake it or glaze it according to the paint manufacturer's directions.

Glass Fact

APOTHECARY GLASS: These glass bottles, vials, and other containers were first mass produced around the first century A.D. and used for storing medicine or medicinal ingredients.

Form-Fitting Votive

Use a light touch to wrap your paint around sculpted or molded forms, and you end up with a positively graceful piece of colored glass. This very sweet votive, in shimmering shades of pink and green, is an elegant example of less is more, simple is better.

DESIGNER: Casey Phillips

What You Need

Sculpted glass votive

Glass paints in ruby and olive green

Fine-to-medium artist's brushes

What You Do

1. Wash and prepare the glass surface.

2. Apply thin layers of paint to the edges of your votive's sculpted design, choosing and varying your colors according to what the design suggests. In the project shown, the designer used ruby on the petal-like panels and rim, then applied olive green to the shoots rising up from the base.

3. Once the paint is thoroughly dry, bake it or glaze it according to the paint manufacturer's directions.

Polka Dot Coffee Mugs

You've followed someone's healthful advice and switched to decaf. Still, you want something about that first cup in the morning to perk you up. A set of mugs like this will take you from groggy to on the ball in no time.

DESIGNER: Billie Worrell

What You Need

4 Irish coffee mugs

Shimmery-finish glass paints in purple, gold, emerald green, and orange

Artist's brushes (#4 round and ¾-inch [1.9 cm] wash/glaze)

Compressed sponge

Ruler

Pencil

Sturdy scissors

Paper towels

What You Do

1. Wash and prepare the glass surfaces.

2. Paint the bases and stems of the mugs, using a different one of the four colors for each. Use a clean, dry wash/glaze brush each time you switch colors. Let this base layer of paint dry completely.

3. If the stems of your mugs have grooves, use the round brush to paint the indentations in accent colors (painting on top of the base layer of paint). Paint orange grooves on the purple stems, purple grooves on the orange stems, green grooves on the gold stems, and gold grooves on the green stems. Use a clean, dry brush each time you switch colors.

4. Cut four circles from the compressed sponge, each approximately ¾ inch (1.9 cm) in diameter.

5. Dampen all the circles, then remove the excess water by squeezing them in paper towels.

6. Using one sponge circle per color, dab dots of paint on the bodies of the mugs, covering each with dots of all four colors.

7. Once the paint is thoroughly dry, bake it or glaze it according to the paint manufacturer's directions.

Pitcher with Swirls and Stripes

It's fanciful yet functional—and oh, so cool. This is the kind of pitcher that puts you on nonstop alert for any opportunity to pour someone a glass of water.

DESIGNER: Shelley Lowell

What You Need

Frosted glass pitcher (In the project shown, the designer used a frosted cobalt blue pitcher.)

Pencil and paper (optional)

Glass paints in yellow, blue, red, and orange

Chisel-shaped artist's brushes

Lazy Susan or cake stand (optional) (Either device will make painting designs that continue all the way around the body of the pitcher easier.)

What You Do

1. Wash and prepare the glass surface.

2. If you like, draw a sketch for the pattern you'll paint so you can refer to it as you work. You may even want to transfer your pattern to the pitcher.

• Begin with two wavy lines running in a tilted ring around the body of the pitcher. The space between the wavy lines can widen and narrow as the lines move around the pitcher.

• Add three parallel stripes running between the spots where the handle connects to the pitcher, down to the base, and back up to their starting point. As with the wavy lines, the spaces between the stripes can widen and narrow as they move around the pitcher.

• Finish with tiny circles covering the surface of the pitcher outside of the swirls and stripes.

3. Paint on one color at a time, using a new brush (or cleaning and drying the same brush) each time you switch colors. If you want an opaque look, you

Glass Fact

Depression glass isn't glass that's feeling a little down, but rather a type of inexpensive glass manufactured during the 1920s and '30s that's extremely popular among collectors today. It was generally machine-made tableware and kitchenware available in a wide variety of colors. Often, Depression glass was given away as a promotional item. You could get it in breakfast cereals, sacks of flour, and with a fast-food meal or a tank of gas. Not all glass made during the '20s and '30s is considered Depression glass; higher quality pressed glass made during the period is called *elegant glass.*

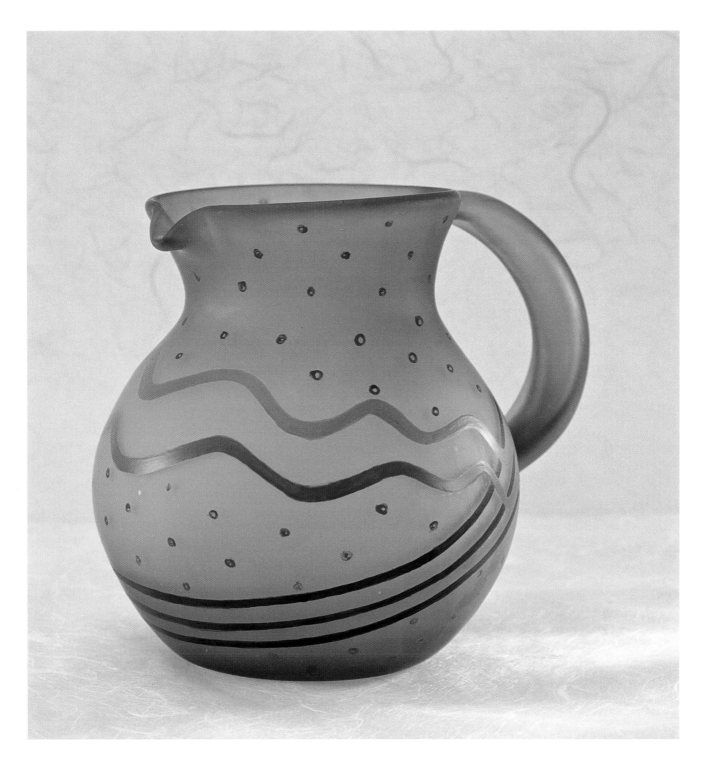

may need to apply several coats of paint, letting the paint dry completely between coats. Begin with yellow on the top wavy line and orange on the bottom one.

4. Paint the stripes in blue, breaking where they meet the swirls.

5. Add the small circles in red.

6. Once the paint is thoroughly dry, bake it or glaze it according to the paint manufacturer's directions.

Petite Party Favors

Paint these dainty vials in a translucent shade, add gold accents, then fill them with essential oils, lucky charms, or rolled up scrolls of poetry. Perfect for those times you need to give someone "a little something."

DESIGNER: Kelly McMullen

What You Need

Small glass vials with lids (Check craft stores and scientific supply stores. The vials shown measure 1⅞ inches [4.7 cm] in length and ½ inch [1.3 cm] in diameter.)

Translucent glass paints in pink, purple, and aqua (or other colors you like)

Outliner (gold)

Artist's brush (#12 flat)

Wooden skewers

Sheet of polystyrene foam

What You Do

1. Wash and prepare the glass surfaces.

2. Paint the vials with even strokes, holding each on the end of a finger as you work. As you finish painting each vial, slide a skewer inside it and stick the other end of the skewer into the polystyrene. Leave the painted vials to dry on the ends of the skewers.

3. Once the vials are dry, add accents of stars, dots, spirals, and other shapes with the gold outliner. Figure 1 provides several options to follow as a guide.

4. Once the paint is thoroughly dry, bake it or glaze it according to the paint manufacturer's directions.

Figure 1

Colored Bottle Set

If you don't know where to begin, choose a piece of colored glass to start with and let it be your guide. Here's a three-part look at the brilliant results of playing with various shades.

DESIGNER: Diana Light

What You Need

3 glass bottles in different solid colors

Glass paints in shades darker than or in contrast to the colors of the bottles (For the project shown, the designer chose deep green for the pale green bottle, bright yellow-orange for the yellow bottle, and turquoise plus silver accent paint for the light blue bottle.)

Carbon paper and pen

Artist's brushes (both round and fine)

Patterns for these designs appear on page 121.

What You Do

1. Wash and prepare the glass surfaces.

2. Use carbon paper to transfer the patterns on page 121 to the bottles. Transfer random spirals and star bursts to one bottle, varying the size and direction of the spirals. Transfer stars to another, making them somewhat smaller as they move up the neck of the bottle. Transfer leaves (some with vein lines), seeds, and berries to the third, putting larger leaves at the bottom of the bottle and being careful not to over-crowd the images in general.

3. Paint the patterns in the colors you have chosen for each bottle. On the bottle featuring stars, fill in some of the stars and outline half of the others with an accent color, such as the silver in the project shown, to create a "shadow" effect.

4. Once the paint is thoroughly dry, bake it or glaze it according to the paint manufacturer's directions.

Galactic Globe Light

Know a kid who would flip over the idea of lighting
a room with spaceships, shooting stars, and other
cool, cosmic stuff? Here's a bright, colorful way to
make any budding astronaut's day.

DESIGNER: Diana Light

What You Need

White globe (like those sold in hardware stores to attach to ceiling fan lights)
Opaque glass paints in bright blue, purple, yellow-orange, red, and silver
Water-based marker
Carbon paper and pen
Small, round artist's brush
Patterns for this design appear on page 123.

Glass Fact

You think *you've* got it tough at work! Venetian glass was so popular during the 15th to 18th centuries in Europe that the government enacted strict regulations concerning the behavior of its celebrated Murano glassmakers. Not only were they under orders never to reveal the secrets of their trade, the Muranese artisans were also forbidden to leave the country under penalty of death. Those who attempted harrowing nighttime escapes were often chased by hired assassins. (Despite—or possibly because of—these laws, many eventually managed to flee Venice and set up glassworks elsewhere in Europe.)

What You Do

1. Wash and prepare the glass surface.

2. With the water-based marker, draw a spiral around the globe. Begin at the center of the base, making the spiral tight at first, then widening it to just a couple of rotations as it moves up the globe.

3. Use carbon paper to transfer the patterns for shooting stars, comets, planets, and other images on page 123 to the surface of the globe. You may want some of the images to overlap the spiral. If so, use water and a cotton swab to erase those portions of the spiral.

4. Begin painting the images in bright combinations of the paint colors listed above, using the project photo as a guide. Allow base colors to dry completely before you add outlines, dots, spirals, or other accents to any image.

5. Once the images are dry, paint the spiral. Start by painting it with a thick, bold band of blue. Let the blue paint dry completely. Then, add a matching band of yellow-orange beside it.

6. Once the paint is thoroughly dry, bake it or glaze it according to the paint manufacturer's directions.

Flashy Flutes

This eye-catching design was inspired by the object's "architecture." The flutes that run around the pitcher provide ready-made sections, each waiting for its own embellishment.

DESIGNER: Shelley Lowell

What You Need

Fluted glass pitcher

Pearlized or shimmering glass paints in green, blue, raspberry, orange, and white

Paint palette or plastic lids

Glaze

Chisel-shaped artist's brushes

What You Do

1. Wash and prepare the glass surface.

2. Paint every other flute a solid color, alternating green, blue, raspberry, and orange. For an opaque look, you'll need to apply several coats, letting the paint dry between coats.

3. Once the solid bands of color are dry, paint a simple design of "doodles" on each with white paint. Use the detail photos shown here as inspiration. You can create combinations of squares and circles, dots and dashes, spirals and squiggles, or any other freehand pattern you like. (For tiny dots, use the handle end of your brush dipped in paint.) The white paint acts as a base for the color you will add to the doodles in the next step. It saves you from having to add several coats of color and prevents the base color of the solid band from showing through on the surface design.

4. On the paint palette or in plastic lids, mix a little glaze with each of the colors you'll use to paint the surface design you created in step 3. The glaze adds a bit of transparency to the paint.

5. Paint over the white doodles in any color combinations you like, referring to the project shown as a guide.

6. Once the paint is dry, add a coat of glaze to each painted band, let it dry, then add a second coat.

Holiday Balls

Whether you hang them from green garland accented with tiny white lights, arrange them art-fully in cut-crystal bowls, or add velvet ribbon and give them as gifts, these beautiful glass bulbs add high style to the holidays.

DESIGNER: Megan Kirby

What You Need

    Round glass ornaments

    Outliner in gold and white (Paint pens and fabric paint, which comes in tubes, also work well for this project.)

    Scissors

    Water-based marker (optional)

    Fishing line or ribbon

What You Do

1. Wash and prepare the glass surfaces.

2. When you snip the tip off the outliner applicator tube, cut as close to the end as possible. Doing so will allow for a thin stream of outliner, which gives you better control when you're applying it.

3. Choose a simple, repeating pattern, and apply the outliner. The balls shown feature a large spiral, small and large polka dots, a simple paisley shape sur-rounded by polka dots, and a dripping layer of melt-ing "snow." Though uncomplicated is better for these non-fussy balls, you may want to draw your design on first with the water-based marker, so you have a pat-tern to follow as you apply the outliner. If you'd like to apply tiny dots of color inside larger polka dots (such as the gold dots inside the white polka dots on the ball with the paisley shape), paint the polka dots first, let them dry completely, then add the smaller dots. Gravity helps a lot if you're after the melting snow effect. Simply apply lots of outliner and let it drip.

4. Once the paint is thoroughly dry, bake it or glaze it according to the paint manufacturer's directions.

5. If you wish, add fishing line or ribbon as hangers.

Champagne Flutes

These cheery party glasses have celebration painted all over them—right down to the effervescent little bubbles. They're perfect for toasting everything from a new year to a new job to a new bottle of champagne.

DESIGNER: Katheryn M. Smolski

What You Need

Clear glass champagne flutes

Translucent glass paints in red and blue

Outliner (gold)

Artist's brushes (pointed)

What You Do

1. Wash and prepare the glass surfaces.

2. Fill a brush with red paint and begin painting your first glass. Make quick, light, upward strokes from the top of the stem up the glass about 1½ to 2 inches (3.8 to 5 cm). Lift the brush gradually as you move it up the glass.

3. Repeat the process, painting half of the glasses in your set red. Then, with a clean, dry brush, paint the rest of the glasses in the set in the same way with blue paint. Allow all of the glasses to dry completely.

4. With the gold outliner, make tiny, light dots in a random pattern over and slightly above the colored strokes.

5. Once the paint is thoroughly dry, bake it or glaze it according to the paint manufacturer's directions.

Plate in Full Bloom

Buy the right piece of glass to start with, and a plate this stunning is as easy as painting inside the lines. The designer started with a plate that featured a floral pattern in the glass, then she brought it to life with vivid colors.

DESIGNER: Kay Crane

What You Need

Plate with floral design in the glass

Glass paints in yellow, orange, scarlet, olive, and emerald

Artist's brushes

Glass Fact

Glasswort is the common name for any of several plants (genera Salicornia and Salsola) of the goosefoot family, often found in saline or coastal desert areas and characterized by fleshy stems and rudimentary, scaly leaves. Their ash, which is rich in soda, was once used in making glass and soap.

What You Do

1. Wash and prepare the glass surface.

2. Painting on the back side of the plate, brush several coats of yellow on the flowers, letting the paint dry thoroughly between each coat.

3. Once the yellow reaches the intensity of color your want, add orange to the center of the petals, and blend it out to the edges.

4. Give the centers of each petal a scarlet highlight to add a feeling of depth to your design.

5. The plate in the project shown features both leaves and a ribbon that swirls out from the center. The designer painted the leaves olive, then added a touch of emerald. She painted the ribbon emerald, fading the color out toward the edges of the plate.

6. Bake or glaze the plate, according to the paint manufacturer's directions.

Powder Room Set

The soft, matt finish of frosted glass provides a pretty backdrop for translucent rosebuds decorated with gold. Paint several pieces, such as the lotion bottle, cotton ball canister, and soap dish shown here, and your shimmering set will beautify any bathroom.

DESIGNER: Kelly McMullen

What You Need

Frosted glass pieces (soap dishes, lotion bottles, canisters, etc.)

Carbon paper and pen

Glass paints in fuchsia and green

Outliner (gold)

Artist's brush (#6 round)

The pattern for this design appears on page 123.

What You Do

1. Wash and prepare the glass surfaces.

2. With the carbon paper and pen, transfer the rose pattern on page 123 in a random fashion to the surface of your frosted glass pieces. Add a leaf on each side of some roses; on others, trace only one leaf.

3. Paint the irregular bloom shapes first, using fuchsia paint and the #6 round brush. Let the paint dry completely.

4. With a clean, dry brush, paint the leaves green. Let the paint dry completely.

5. Use the gold outliner to outline each rose and leaf. Add highlight lines inside each, using the pattern as a guide.

6. Add small gold dots sparingly between the roses on each piece.

7. Once the paint is thoroughly dry, bake it or glaze it according to the paint manufacturer's directions.

Glass Fact

GLASSY-EYED: The opposite of the expression you'd want to see on the face of a client or a date after dazzling him or her with your sparkling conversation. Coined by someone who considered glass dull and lifeless, the term is used to describe a flat, expressionless, zoned-out stare.

Spring Table Set

Create this retro-look set by layering a couple of sponged-on colors over a simple stencil. Then give it a home on any table that's happy with vintage flair.

DESIGNER: Casey Phillips

What You Need

Clear glass table set (The project shown features a
sugar bowl, a cream pitcher, a butter dish, and oil
and vinegar cruets.)

Translucent glass paints in blue and yellow

Outliner (black)

Scissors or craft knife

Artist's brushes (medium and fine)

Sponges

The pattern for this design appears on page 122.

Glass Fact

Glass meant big money—and
a bit of eccentricity—for
some. Between 1763 and
1774, German businessman
Henry Steigel operated a
large glassworks in Manheim,
Pennsylvania. He made so
much money that he styled
himself as a baron, going so
far as to hire musicians to
play anytime he pulled up at
home in his coach. He
spread some of the wealth
around, too, loaning the land
for Manheim's Lutheran
church and asking that rent
be paid in the form of a single
red rose per year. (Steigel's
descendants still receive the
agreed-upon rent today. The
rose is always delivered during the second week in June.)

What You Do

1. Wash and prepare the glass surfaces.

2. Make multiple copies of the daisy pattern on page
122, creating enough flower shapes to cover your glass
pieces. Since you'll be placing the stencils on top of
wet paint, you won't be able to reuse them, so cut as
many as you need to complete the set. For the set
shown, the designer used 24 daisy shapes. You'll also
need to enlarge and adapt some petal shapes to circle
the lid of the sugar bowl, if yours has one.

3. Work on one piece at a time. Wet a sponge,
squeeze out the excess water, load it with yellow paint,
and sponge the first piece until you have complete
and even coverage.

4. While the paint is still wet, place the paper flowers where you want your flower images to be. The wet
paint will hold them in place.

5. Wet a second sponge, squeeze out the excess
water, and cover the surface of the piece (including
the paper flowers) with blue.

6. While the paint is still wet, peel off the paper
flowers, using the tip of the craft knife to help start
the peeling process, if necessary.

7. Repeat steps 2 through 5 until all of the pieces in
your set have been sponged with yellow and blue
paint. Let the paint dry completely.

8. Outline the flower shapes and centers with
black outliner.

9. With a brush, paint the flower centers blue
or yellow.

10. Paint over any handles or knobs you want to
have additional color. You may choose to paint the
stopper on the oil cruet blue, for example, and the
stopper on the vinegar cruet yellow.

11. Once the paint is thoroughly dry, bake it or glaze
it according to the paint manufacturer's directions.

Painted Window Room Divider

In this age of multiprocessing, when work spaces and living spaces often blend into one big mass of pillows, paperwork, and dishes, who couldn't use an artful way to section off one nook from another? Here, the designers latched onto the hot home decorating trend of giving old windows facelifts and new functions. They created a work-of-art divider, perfect for everything from countertops to cubicles.

DESIGNERS: Amy Cook & Les Caison III

What You Need

Multipaned window

Opaque glass paints in peach, royal blue, lavender, lemon yellow, light green, red, pink, dark green, light blue, orange, pale yellow, and plum

Tape

Artist's brushes (large and medium)

Patterns for this design appear on page 124.

What You Do

1. If possible, remove the panes of glass from your window frame. Doing so will make painting easier—and keep the frame free of unwanted drips and splatters of paint.

Glass Fact

CARNIVAL GLASS: First produced in 1908, this glass is characterized by an iridescent coating that creates a rainbow effect. When its popularity dropped off in the 1920s, it became a standard carnival prize—hence its name.

---

2. Clean and prepare the glass panes.

3. Make photocopies of the patterns on page 124. Tape one to the front of each pane, so the patterns show through on the back (which is the side you'll be painting on). The patterns will serve as guides as you paint.

4. Paint the interior of each seed symbol first by simply "coloring" inside the lines. You can follow the pattern order and the color selections that are featured in the project shown, or you can vary the order and/or assign the colors differently. If you'd like to exactly replicate the design shown, paint the symbols in a clockwise fashion, starting with the pane that will be in the upper left-hand corner. Paint the first symbol royal blue, the second lemon yellow, the third red, the fourth dark green, the fifth orange, and the sixth plum. Let the paint dry.

5. Once the symbols are completely dry, paint the backgrounds of each pane. (Painting right over the dried symbols is fine, since the finished design will be viewed from the other side of the windowpane.) Again, if you want to exactly replicate the design shown, paint in the same clockwise fashion. Paint the first background peach, the second lavender, the third light green, the fourth pink, the fifth light blue, and the sixth pale yellow. Let the paint dry.

6. Remove the pattern pieces and place each pane back in its spot in the window frame.

Floral Doorknobs

Spot an ordinary object sporting an unexpected dash of embellishment, and it can make your day (or at least cause you to crack a smile). These pretty painted doorknobs make opening the linen closet, letting the cat out, and loads of other everyday chores much happier tasks.

DESIGNER: Casey Phillips

What You Need

- Glass doorknob (sold at hardware stores as replacement knobs)
- Glass paints in various colors (Purple, yellow, pink, white, green, and black are shown here.)
- Assorted artist's brushes (medium to fine)

What You Do

1. Wash and prepare the glass surface, then paint a flower that appeals to you—maybe one that matches the wallpaper or that looks like the real thing blooming outside the window. Three are featured here.

Iris

Load a brush with purple, and paint four to six strokes spreading out from the center of the knob. While the purple is still wet, add a dollop of yellow to the base of each purple stroke, and allow it to flow. Add four small strokes of green, equally placed, around the outer edge of the knob.

Lily of the Valley

Paint three long green stems on the center of the knob. Let the paint dry. Along the edge of each stem, paint three or four white blossoms. Start by painting a dot. Then pull the brush down to form a bell shape with the white paint. Let the paint dry, then use a fine brush to outline the blossoms and stems in black.

Rose

If you'd like to follow a rough guide for this flower, use the outline of the rose pattern on page 123. Paint pink petal shapes in the center of the knob and a small bud just below the bloom. Let the paint dry. Add green stems and leaves. Let the paint dry, then use a fine brush to outline the petals, stems, and leaves in black.

2. Once the paint is thoroughly dry, bake it or glaze it according to the paint manufacturer's directions.

Poppy Pitcher

~

Leave this pitcher absolutely empty, and it will still look radiant, with its vibrant field of poppies rising up around the base. Better yet, fill it with a spray of the real thing for a breathtaking centerpiece. With a pattern as your guide, creating one is as easy as filling in the lines with a brilliant blend of colors.

DESIGNER: Diana Light

What You Need

Clear glass pitcher

Glass paints in 3 shades of green, 3 shades of red-orange, purple, and black

Outliner (black) (optional)

Tape

Artist's brushes (round and fine liner)

Patterns for this design appear on page 124.

What You Do

1. Wash and prepare the glass surface.

2. Make multiple copies of the poppy pattern on page 124, and tape overlapping arrangements of flowers, buds, stems, and leaves to the inside of the pitcher to follow as a guide, with the largest blossoms near the top of the pitcher. (As an alternative, you can copy images you like from magazines or books and use them as patterns.)

3. Using either black outliner or black paint and the fine-liner brush, outline the entire pattern, and let it dry completely.

4. With the round brush, paint the leaves and stems, using the lightest shade of green on those in the foreground, the medium shade on those in the middle, and the darkest shade on those in the background. Let them dry completely.

5. Using a clean, dry round brush, paint the flowers and buds, using the lightest shade of red-orange on those in the foreground, the medium shade on those

in the middle, and the darkest shade on those in the background. Let them dry completely.

6. Paint the centers of the flowers purple, using a clean, dry round brush.

7. When the flower centers are dry, add any details you like (such as the stamen and pistils in the project shown) with black paint and the fine-liner brush.

8. Once the paint is thoroughly dry, bake it or glaze it according to the paint manufacturer's directions.

Fresh as a Daisy Lemonade Set

A set as refreshing as this one has the power to send you rushing to the kitchen to start squeezing lemons immediately. Paint your own, then position it poolside for months of heat relief.

DESIGNER: Kim Ballor

What You Need

Clear glass pitcher and a set of 4 glasses

Glass paints in white, yellow, and light blue

¼-inch (6 mm) painter's tape or masking tape cut to size

Small flat artist's brush and medium round artist's brush

What You Do

1. Wash and prepare the glass surfaces.

2. At the top of the pitcher, place five strips of tape running horizontally, one tape width (¼ inch or 6 mm) apart. Place four strips of tape in the same pattern at the top of each glass. Press the tape firmly in place.

3. Using the small, flat brush, apply light blue paint to the taped area, staying within the top and bottom strips of tape.

4. Carefully remove the tape while the paint is wet.

5. When the paint is completely dry, place strips of tape vertically all the way around the same area of the pitcher and each glass, again spacing it one tape width (¼ inch or 6 mm) apart.

6. Again, cover the area with light blue paint, carefully remove the tape while the paint is wet, and let the paint dry completely.

7. Paint daisies to cover the bottom of the pitcher and the glasses. Begin each by using the flat brush to paint a yellow circle approximately ¼ inch (6 mm) in diameter. For the petals, load the round brush with a good amount of white paint. Start about 1 inch (2.5 cm) away from the yellow center, press the brush to the glass, and drag it toward the center, lifting it to a point just before it reaches the center. Make six or seven petals for each daisy; they don't all have to be identical.

8. Use the handle of the brush dipped in yellow to print a few dots on the background between the daisies.

9. Once the paint is thoroughly dry, bake it or glaze it according to the paint manufacturer's directions.

Glass Fact

STAINED GLASS: Stained glass is glass that has been painted and then fired. It's usually pieced together with lead channels and used to make objects such as lamp shades, hanging pieces, and, of course, windows. The practice began around the fifth century A.D., but didn't reach its height of popularity until the Middle Ages, when stained glass was used to adorn cathedral windows.

Fluted Platter

*Splashy, layered-on colors and clever use of a combing tool make
a plate that's pretty enough to leave on permanent display.*

DESIGNER: Kathy Cooper

What You Need

Large glass platter with a fluted edge

Glass paints in citrus yellow, tangerine, fuchsia,
apple-candy green, mulberry, and turquoise

Artist's brushes (thin; wide and flat)

Rubber combing tool

The pattern for this design appears on page 122.

What You Do

1. Wash and prepare the glass surface.

2. You'll paint this entire design in "reverse" on the outside of the platter. Turn the platter over and begin by using the thin brush to add yellow stripes along the flutes of the platter's edge. Let the paint dry.

3. With the wide, flat brush, paint two sections with fuchsia paint, skip two sections, paint two more, and so on until you've circled the platter.

4. Drag the combing tool through each section, and let the paint dry.

5. Paint the remaining sections with turquoise, and drag the combing tool through each, then let the paint dry.

6. If you'd like to follow a pattern, make multiple copies of the one for vines on page 122, tape them in a random fashion on the front of the center of the plate, then turn the plate back over and follow the patterns as you paint.

7. Use both green and yellow paint for the vines, applying them with the thin brush and blending them as you add them.

8. With a clean, flat brush, paint green behind the pink flutes. Let the paint dry.

9. In a similar fashion, paint tangerine behind the turquoise flutes.

10. Add irregular blossoms to the vines with the mulberry paint, then let them dry.

11. Paint the center of the plate tangerine.

12. Once the paint is thoroughly dry, bake it or glaze it according to the paint manufacturer's directions.

Glass Fact

It's hard. It takes on solid form. And heaven knows it's breakable. But glass is technically a super-cooled liquid rather than a solid. It's made of molten sand and other elements that cool but don't crystallize. Even though the molecules gain enough cohesion to become rigid and breakable, glass in its hardened form retains whatever shape it had as a liquid.

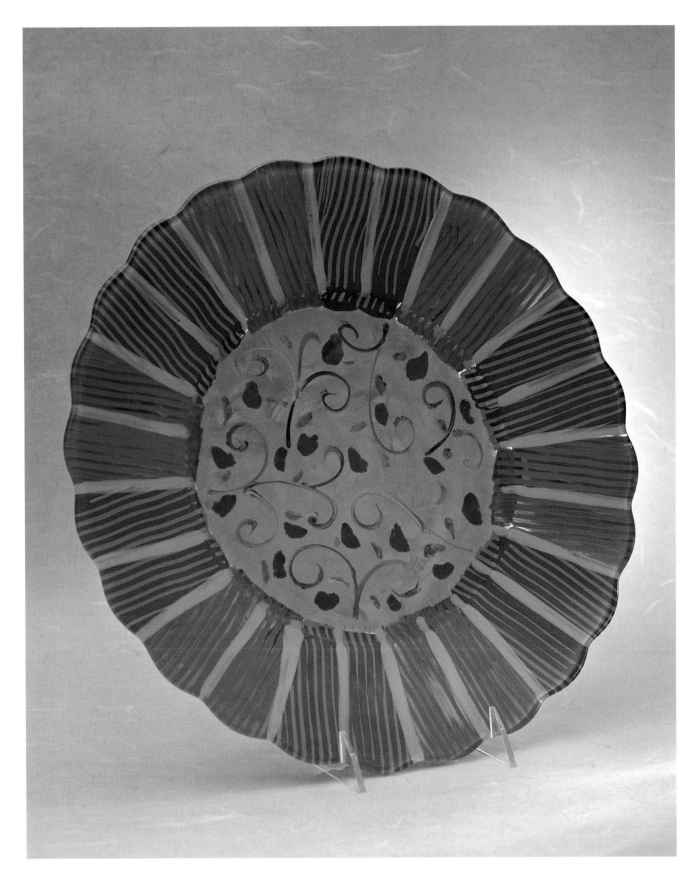

Garden Party Lights

String these buzzing, blooming bulbs around a porch railing or an arbor, plug 'em in, and you've got instant festivity, whether there's a party in progress or not.

DESIGNER: Kim Ballor

What You Need

> **String of outdoor lights with white bulbs**
>
> **Opaque glass paints in raspberry, yellow, black, green, and red**
>
> **Fine metal tip to fit your bottle of black paint (As an alternative, you can use black outliner.)**
>
> **Carbon paper and pen (optional)**
>
> **Small round artist's brush**
>
> **Flat sheet of polystyrene foam**
>
> **Patterns for this design appear on page 123.**

What You Do

1. Unscrew the bulbs from their bases and separate them into three groups. You'll paint flowers on one group, bumblebees on another, and ladybugs on the third. You can transfer the patterns on page 123 to the bulbs first, or simply use the illustrations as guides and paint the images freehand.

Flowers

Paint several flowers on the surface of each bulb in this group, beginning with a yellow center, then adding five raspberry petals and one or two green leaves on each. With the metal-tipped bottle of black paint or the black outliner, loosely outline the flowers and petals.

Bumblebees

Paint several bumblebees on the surface of each bulb in this group. Start with the yellow bodies. Once the bodies are completely dry, add a black head, stripes, and antennae to each bee. With the metal-tipped bot-

tle of black paint or the black outliner, outline two wings on each side of each bee.

Ladybugs

Paint several ladybugs on the surface of each bulb in this group. Start each by making a red circle. At the bottom of the circle, extend two small tails. Let the bodies dry completely. Then, with black, paint a head and dots on each ladybug. Add the metal tip to the bottle of black paint or use black outliner to outline each ladybug loosely.

2. Paint one bulb at a time, keeping in mind that a generous coat of paint will give you the best look when the bulbs are lit. When you finish with each, sink its base into the sheet of polystyrene so it stays upright as it dries.

3. After the paint has dried at least 48 hours, screw the bulbs back into their bases and party away.

Hanging Vase

~

Find a delightful little hanging vessel like this one (or wrap some wire around a bottle to create one yourself), hang it in a window, and you've got a bud vase and sun catcher all in one.

DESIGNER: Diana Light

What You Need

Clear glass hanging vase

Translucent glass paints in yellow, orange, scarlet, turquoise, green, and blue

Outliner (gold)

Carbon paper and pen

Artist's brushes (fine liner)

Patterns for this design appear on page 121.

What You Do

1. Wash and prepare the glass surface.

2. Use carbon paper to transfer the patterns on page 121 to the vase. Place flowers around the bottom half. Fill in around the base with sunbursts and small butterflies. Put several large butterflies at the top of the vase, just below the neck, and add a few small butterflies on the neck.

3. Outline the design with the gold outliner, and let it dry completely.

4. Paint the outlined images, using the fine-line brush. Paint the flower stems and leaves green, the petals blue, and the centers turquoise. Alternate scarlet, orange, and yellow paint on the sunbursts. Use yellow and orange on the large butterfly wings and red on the large butterfly bodies.

5. Once the paint is thoroughly dry, bake it or glaze it according to the paint manufacturer's directions.

Bowl of Flowers and Dots

*An elaborate (but easy!) process of layering colors and tex-
tures on the outside of a plain glass bowl makes the inside
come alive. Use the technique to turn any ordinary dish
into a vivid centerpiece.*

DESIGNER: Kathy Cooper

What You Need

Large glass bowl

Opaque glass paints in citrus yellow, tangerine, fuchsia, apple-candy green, mulberry, and turquoise

Artist's brushes (thin; wide and flat)

Rubber combing tool

Paint eraser

The pattern for this design appears on page 121.

What You Do

1. Wash and prepare the glass surface.

2. Painting on the outside of the bowl, use the wide, flat brush to create a random series of approximately four wide mulberry stripes.

3. While the paint is still wet, drag the combing tool through each stripe to accent it with a series of long lines. Let the paint dry completely.

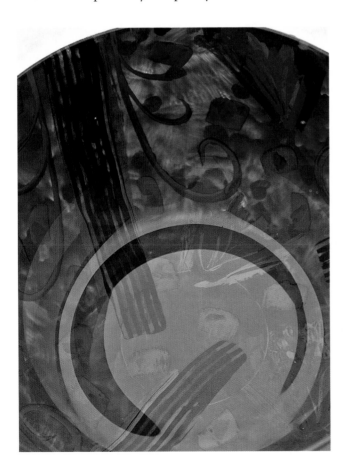

4. If you'd like to follow a pattern, make copies of the swirls on page 121 and tape them to the inside of the bowl so that they border each purple stripe, using the project photo as a guide. On the outside of the bowl, paint the swirls tangerine with the thin brush. Let the paint dry.

5. Use a clean, dry wide brush to paint fan-shaped flowers in fuchsia on the outside of the bottom and sides of the bowl. Simply shape your brush strokes in a triangular formation to create the random flowers.

6. While the paint is still wet, use the paint eraser to scratch accent lines in the center of each flower, using the project photo as a guide. Let the paint dry.

7. With a clean, dry flat brush, paint yellow over the scratch lines in the flowers, extending your paint strokes beyond the flower edges a bit. Let the paint dry.

8. With a clean, dry flat brush, paint apple-candy green extending past the edges of the pink flowers.

9. While the paint is still wet, use the paint eraser to scratch lines in the green. Let the paint dry.

10. With the same brush, add a layer of candy-apple green behind the mulberry stripes, extending past the side edges.

11. With a clean, dry brush, paint "messy" fuchsia dots randomly all over the bowl. Let the paint dry.

12. Clean the brush and use it to add strokes of mulberry and apple-candy green along the rim of the bowl.

13. Add splashes of tangerine over the pink dots. Let the paint dry.

14. Paint the entire outside of the bowl turquoise. Let the paint dry.

15. Add yellow dots over the turquoise paint.

16. Once the paint is thoroughly dry, bake it or glaze it according to the paint manufacturer's directions.

Alpine Hot Chocolate Mugs

Paint a pair (or more) of these cozy mugs. Each time you fill them with steaming chocolate, your guests will swear you plucked them from the cupboard of a chalet in the Swiss Alps.

DESIGNER: Dorris Sorensen

What You Need

Clear glass mugs

Opaque glass paints in light blue, maize, deep coral, and hunter green

Scissors and tape or carbon paper and pen

Artist's brushes (#8 flat, #1 liner)

Small cosmetic sponge

The pattern for this design appears on page 121.

Glass Fact

CRANBERRY GLASS: This pinkish-red glass is made by adding gold chloride to the glass mixture. The Romans first developed the secret formula, which was lost when the Roman empire fell and then reinvented in Bohemia in the 1600s. Since it's both expensive and difficult to produce, most items that appear to be cranberry glass today are actually made from regular glass that has been only thinly coated with actual cranberry glass.

What You Do

1. Wash and prepare the glass surfaces.

2. Transfer the pattern on page 121 to the front of each mug by either taping a copy inside or tracing it onto the surfaces with carbon paper.

3. Use the #8 flat brush to paint the outside of each flower petal light blue. Let the paint dry completely.

4. With a clean, dry #8 flat brush, paint the inside of each petal maize, then add a coral center to the flower.

5. Add a freehand leaf stroke in hunter green between each of the petals with a clean, dry #8 flat brush.

6. Use the same leaf stroke to paint a chain around the center of each mug. Each chain should run from one side of the flower around to the other side.

7. With a #1 liner brush, add an accent of maize paint above each leaf stroke of each chain.

8. Repeat the green-and-yellow chain design around the base of each mug.

9. With a clean, dry #1 liner brush, paint a wavy line of blue below the rim of each mug.

10. Add a wavy line of coral below each blue line with a clean, dry #1 liner brush.

11. With the same brush, paint a line of small dots (to mirror the center of each flower) just below the chain design circling the center of each mug.

12. Use a clean, dry #1 liner brush to add groupings of three thin dashes above the wavy lines at the top of each mug.

13. Dip the small cosmetic sponge in coral, and use it to coat the edge of the base of each mug with paint.

14. Once the paint is thoroughly dry, bake it or glaze it according to the paint manufacturer's directions.

Morning Glory Plate

With the rich, ornamental look of fine stained glass, this decorative plate deserves to be displayed alongside your other artistic showpieces.

DESIGNER: Sally Rhett

What You Need

Clear glass plate

Outliner or liquid leading

Glass paints in yellow, green, blue, and purplish pink

Artist's brushes

The pattern for this design appears on page 122.

What You Do

1. Wash and prepare the glass surface.

2. Place a copy of the pattern on page 122 under the plate to follow as a guide.

3. Use outliner or leading to draw the pattern on the front of the plate and to make the simple dot-and-dash border around the rim. Allow the outlined pattern to dry completely.

4. With a brush, fill in the center circle with yellow and the leaves with green.

5. Paint the flower blossoms blue. While the paint is still wet, blend in the purplish-pink paint at the base of each blossom.

6. Once the paint is thoroughly dry, bake it or glaze it according to the paint manufacturer's directions.

Hot Tamale Garden Votives

Turn the heat up at your next patio party with this spicy set of candleholders. Stake them in the ground, strike a match, and watch the sparks fly.

DESIGNER: Travis Waldron

What You Need

Glass votive holders with staked bases

Glass paints in burgundy, dark green, black, and gold

Scissors

Tape

Artist's brushes (#6 round and #2 fine)

The pattern for this design appears on page 124.

What You Do

1. Wash and prepare the glass surfaces.

2. Make multiple copies of the pepper pattern on page 124, and tape them inside your votive holders to follow as guides while you paint. In the project shown, the designer placed four peppers evenly around the base of each holder.

3. Working on the outside of the holder, paint the pepper shapes in burgundy using the #6 brush, and allow the paint to dry completely.

4. With a clean, dry #6 brush, paint the leaves and stem of each pepper in dark green.

5. Use the #2 brush to outline each pepper in black in a random, broken fashion.

6. With a clean, dry #2 brush, apply a stroke of gold accent paint to the body of each pepper. Then, paint a gold band around the top of the holder.

7. Once the paint is thoroughly dry, bake it or glaze it according to the paint manufacturer's directions.

Bubble Bowl

Who needs an official celebration? This high-spirited serving bowl is reason enough—all by itself—for mixing up a sparkling batch of champagne punch or serving imported foil-wrapped chocolates.

DESIGNER: Kim Ballor

What You Need

Clear glass serving or punch bowl

Peel-off leading circles in various sizes (For a large bowl, purchase 3 packages of circles.)

Glass paint that simulates stained glass when dry, in clear, amethyst, slate blue, emerald green, and magenta

Stencil brush

Cotton swabs

Straight pin

What You Do

1. Wash and prepare the glass surface.

2. Turn the bowl upside down. Begin peeling the self-stick leading circles from their paper packaging and placing them on the bowl. Start at the bottom, placing the biggest concentration of circles there and positioning them close together. Here and there, place smaller circles inside larger circles. As you work up the bowl, place fewer circles and position them farther apart.

3. Apply clear paint to the bowl surface (including the space between the circles), stippling it on (using repeated small touches) with the stencil brush. Use cotton swabs to wipe off any paint that makes its way to the leading circles.

4. Use the four other paint colors to fill in the circles, squeezing the paint straight from the bottles onto the glass. Pop any air bubbles with the straight pin while the paint is still wet.

5. Allow the paint to dry according to the manufacturer's directions.

Cylinder Vase

Start with a striking vase shape that gives you lots of surface area to work with. Follow a surprisingly simple process of applying peel-off leading and combing on paint. The result? A handsome centerpiece vase.

DESIGNER: Kim Ballor

What You Need

Clear cylinder vase

Peel-off leading strips

Glass paint that simulates stained glass when dry, in amethyst, magenta, slate blue, and denim blue

Combing tool with wide teeth

Scissors or craft knife

Cotton swabs

What You Do

1. Wash and prepare the glass surface.

2. Peel the self-stick leading strips from their paper packaging and place them on the glass, forming large, random shapes.

3. As you cover the entire vase in a pattern of shapes, trim the strips with scissors or a craft knife so they touch where the lines come together.

4. Working on one section at a time, squeeze the paint straight from the bottle to cover the space inside the leading. Drag the combing tool across the paint inside the section, creating a row of lines.

5. Continue this process until one side of the vase is painted, alternating your paint color and combing direction in each section. Use cotton swabs to carefully wipe off paint that makes its way onto the leading strips.

6. When the painted side of the vase is dry, repeat the process on the other side.

7. Allow the paint to dry according to the manufacturer's directions.

Patterned Platter

*Simple shapes—those we run across every day—have never looked
so stunning. This handsome platter is a masterful mix of contour
and color. And is it ever easy to paint!*

DESIGNER: Shelley Lowell

What You Need

Frosted glass platter (For the project shown, the designer used a turquoise platter.)

Glass paints in blue, green, red, and orange

Sheet of drawing paper large enough for the platter to fit on

Chisel-shaped artist's brushes

Pencil

Black felt-tip pen (medium to fine tip)

What You Do

1. Wash and prepare the glass surface.

2. Place the platter upside down on the drawing paper. Using the pencil, draw around the rim to make an outline of the platter.

3. Remove the platter. Inside the outline of the platter, sketch the pattern you plan to paint. For the project shown, the designer divided the rim of the platter into four sections, with a slightly wavy line separating each. She then chose simple shapes for each: triangles for one, circles for another, squares for the third, and dashes for the fourth.

4. After sketching your design, go over the outlines with the black felt-tip pen to darken the images of your pattern.

5. Place the platter upside down on the paper again. You should be able to see your pattern through the glass and be ready to paint on the back side of the platter.

6. Paint on one color at a time, using a new brush (or cleaning and drying the same brush) each time you switch colors. If you want an opaque look, you may need to apply several coats of paint, letting the paint dry completely between coats.

• Begin by outlining the triangles in blue, then painting in the background in that section. Add a line of blue dashes along the outside edge of one side of the section. (Use the pattern on the project shown as a guide.)

• Outline the circles in green, then paint in the background of that section. Add a line of green dashes along the outside edge of one side of the section. (Again, use the pattern on the project shown as a guide.)

• Fill in the squares with red and the dashes with orange.

7. Once the paint is thoroughly dry, bake it or glaze it according to the paint manufacturer's directions.

Shades of Blue Glass Set

The designer wanted six glasses that would read as a set, but didn't want to simply paint the same pattern six times. Her solution: She settled on a limited selection of colors and a few basic design elements she could repeat—but vary—from glass to glass.

DESIGNER: Laurey-Faye Long

What You Need

6 tall glasses

Glass paints in black, white, and 2 shades of blue

Painter's tape or masking tape

Paper and pencil (optional)

2 small, soft artist's brushes, 1 fine and 1 round

Glass Fact

THE GLASS MENAGERIE: First play by Tennessee Williams (1911-1983), one of the most influential playwrights of the 20th century (who also wrote such modern classics as *Cat on a Hot Tin Roof*, and *A Streetcar Named Desire*). It premiered on Broadway in 1945, and its name refers to the collection of glass animals cherished by Laura, one of the play's main characters.

What You Do

1. Wash and prepare the glass surfaces.

2. On each glass, separate the surface area into two sections by running tape around the base, below the rim, and somewhere in the middle (though the tape need not run exactly in the middle of each glass).

3. Choose two or three design elements you'll repeat on each glass. The project shown features spirals and rectangles. You may want to sketch design variations on a piece of paper first and transfer them to the glasses to serve as a guide for painting.

4. Place your hand inside one of the glasses and hold it upside down to begin painting it. This makes the process comfortable for your brush hand and allows you to easily turn the glass as you paint.

5. With the round brush, paint one design element all the way around one of the taped-off sections, using one of the colors of blue.

6. Using the same color of blue, repeat this process on the other five glasses, varying the design element each time. For example, you may paint a thin rectangle on the first glass, a curvy rectangle on the second, a fat rectangle on the third, and so on.

7. With a clean, dry round brush, switch to the second color of blue. Paint variations of your second design element in the second taped-off section of each glass.

8. Once both colors of paint are dry, remove the tape.

9. With the fine brush, apply black paint to outline the shapes. Absolute precision isn't necessary; let the outline include unpainted glass from time to time.

10. With a clean, dry fine brush and white paint, add additional highlights or another design element (such as the stars shown in this project) here and there.

11. Once the paint is thoroughly dry, bake it or glaze it according to the paint manufacturer's directions.

Mottled Martini Glasses

Few shapes say fun the way the festive flair of a martini glass does. To create these raucous glasses, the designer let her paintbrush play on that theme.

DESIGNER: Margaret Desmond Dahm

What You Need

Martini glasses

Glass paint in blue

Outliner (black)

Black, fine-tipped water-based marker

Artist's brush

Cotton swabs

What You Do

1. Wash and prepare the glass surfaces.

2. With the water-based marker, marking on the inside of the glass, draw a straight line from the inside center up to the rim. Mark an identical line from the center up to the rim across from the first line, then make two more lines, so the glass is divided into quarters.

3. Still marking on the inside of the glass, draw a square-shaped diamond in one quarter and another in the opposite quarter.

4. On the outside of the glass, paint the outline of each diamond in blue, leaving the inside of the diamond clear. Fill in the rest of those two quarters with blue paint, down to the top of the glass's stem. After filling each area with color, dab the paint with the brush to mottle the finish and obscure any brush strokes. Repeat this process on all the glasses in your set and let them dry completely.

5. With black outliner, starting at the top of the stem of a glass and working upward, paint a row of short, parallel, horizontal dashes up one edge of one

colored quarter. It may help to rest your little finger on the rim of the glass to steady your hand. One end of each dash should be just inside the colored area; the other should venture into the clear quarter next to it. Once you've finished a complete line of dashes, they should resemble a row of stitching. Repeat this process on all "joints" between the colored and clear panels of your glasses.

6. Add vertical rows of dots at the end of each dash in all of the clear panels of glass.

7. Starting at the upper left corner of one of the clear panels of glass, paint a line down from the rim, running along the line of dots, to the middle of the clear panel, where it meets the glass stem. Take that line up along the row of dots on the other side of the panel, and continue it around several more times until you have created a triangular spiral. Repeat this process on all of the clear panels of all of your glasses.

8. Remove the lines you made with the water-based marker on the inside of the glass, using a moistened cotton swab or, if they're stubborn, a bit of nail polish remover.

9. Once the paint is thoroughly dry, bake it or glaze it according to the paint manufacturer's directions.

Italian Espresso Set

This saucy little coffee set has everything but the
caffeine and the homemade biscotti.

DESIGNER: Diana Light

What You Need

Clear glass espresso cups and saucers

Opaque glass paints in black, white, green, and red

Drawing paper

Pencil

Black felt-tip pen

Ruler, scissors, and tape (optional)

Artist's brushes (round and fine line)

Glass Fact

END-OF-DAY GLASS:
Glassworkers often used whatever was left in the pots at the end of the day to make their own items, called end-of-day glass, or "friggers." Sometimes they created ordinary objects to sell or use at home, but more often they made pieces for their own amusement, from walking sticks and pipes to small glass animals. Because they used the leftovers, the glass was often multicolored. Over time, any glass made from several different colors came to be called end-of-day glass.

What You Do

1. Wash and prepare the glass surfaces.

2. Place a saucer upside down on the drawing paper. Using the pencil, draw around the rim to make an outline of the saucer. Then turn the saucer over, and trace around the smaller circle, where the cup will sit.

3. Remove the saucer. On the outline of the saucer, sketch the pattern you plan to paint, making a ring of small, evenly spaced square-like shapes around the inner circle and an offset ring of larger square-like shapes above them. The sides of the shapes will flare outward slightly as they move up.

4. After sketching your design, go over the outlines with the black felt-tip pen to darken the images of your pattern.

5. Place a saucer upside down on the paper again. You should be able to see your pattern through the glass and be ready to paint on the back side of the saucer. With the round brush, paint half of your saucers in this manner using black paint. Paint the other half with white paint.

6. On each of the cups in your set, you'll paint a series of vertical stripes of the same width but varying heights. If you want to follow a guide, cut a strip of drawing paper that will fit inside a cup, draw the striped pattern using the ruler and the pencil, outline the pattern with the black pen, and place it inside the cup so it shows through to the front.

7. With the fine-liner brush, paint the stripes, alternating black, white, green, and red paint. Because each stripe should dry completely before you paint the stripe next to it, you may want to paint all of your black stripes (for example) on all of your cups first, let them dry, then move on to white stripes, and so on.

8. Once the paint is thoroughly dry, bake it or glaze it according to the paint manufacturer's directions.

Circular Thinking

Bright, bold splashes of the colors of summer in a fanciful interplay of bubbles and polka dots. Let iced-tea season begin.

DESIGNER: Dorris Sorensen

What You Need

Clear glass pitcher and goblets

Opaque glass paints in azure blue, fuchsia, and yellow

Carbon paper and pen (optional)

Tape (optional)

Artist's brushes (#8 shader and #1 liner)

Pencil with a new, unused eraser

What You Do

1. Wash and prepare the glass surfaces.

2. If you'd like to follow a guide as you paint, transfer a random pattern of the circle in figure 1 to the bodies of the pitcher and the goblets, using the project photo as a guide for placement. Transfer the pattern either by taping copies inside or by tracing the bubble on the surface with carbon paper. (You'll be following the shape of the outer circle only.)

3. With the #8 shader brush and blue paint, paint large, generous, 1-inch (2.5 cm) circles around the body of the pitcher and the goblets. Let the paint dry completely.

4. Dip the eraser end of the pencil in yellow paint, and use it to make a dot in the center of each blue bubble. Make additional eraser dots, sprinkled randomly, on the glass around the blue bubbles. (Again, use the project photo as a guide for placement.) Let the paint dry completely.

5. Dip the #1 liner brush in fuchsia, and paint large, downward strokes on the right side of the yellow dot in each blue bubble, using figure 1 as a guide.

Figure 1

6. With a clean, dry #8 shader brush, paint the handle of the pitcher fuchsia, then add bold, vertical fuchsia stripes spaced approximately ½ inch (1.3 cm) apart around the pitcher base.

7. Add a similar series of stripes around the edge of the base of each goblet.

8. Once the fuchsia paint is dry, use a clean, dry #1 liner brush to add a yellow squiggly line running in a circle above the stripes on both the pitcher and the goblets.

9. Paint the underside of each goblet base blue.

10. Once the paint is thoroughly dry, bake it or glaze it according to the paint manufacturer's directions.

Glasnost Glasses and Ice Bucket

This diamond-studded set is the coolest of ways to keep small shots of your favorite Russian blend ice cold. You can adapt the design to any bucket and collection of glasses.

DESIGNER: Diana Light

What You Need

Clear glass ice bucket and set of shot glasses

Glass paints in red, white, gold, black, and silver

Drawing paper

Pencil

Ruler

Scissors

Tape

Small, round artist's brushes

Glass Fact

Glass was quite the status symbol in Roman households during the height of the Roman empire. To do without it, explained Seneca, one of the hottest playwrights and philosophers of the day, definitely meant you were down and out. "A person finds himself poor and base," he said, "unless his vaulted ceiling is covered with glass."

What You Do

1. Wash and prepare the glass surfaces.

2. Draw large diamond shapes on the piece of paper. (Those on the project shown have sides that measure approximately 2 inches [5 cm].)

3. Make enough copies of the diamonds so that you can tape two rows of them to the inside of your ice bucket (following the pattern on the project shown) and slide two inside each shot glass. They'll serve as guides while you paint.

4. Paint the diamonds around the base of the bucket first. Outline them carefully with the brush and a thin layer of paint, then fill in their interiors. Alternate red, white, gold, and black paint as you go. Let the paint dry completely.

5. Paint the top row of diamonds on the bucket in the same way, alternating the colors top to bottom and side to side.

6. Add silver dots along the zigzag pattern the diamonds create just below the rim of the bucket.

7. Paint two different-colored diamonds curving around the body of each glass, switching to new color combinations with each glass. As you did with the bucket, use red, white, gold, and black paint.

8. On one side of each glass, repeat the pattern of silver dots in the "valley" shape formed by the diamonds.

9. Once the paint is thoroughly dry, bake it or glaze it according to the paint manufacturer's directions.

Painted Mirror

Crackle medium, paints that simulate stained glass, and a basic, bold design turn an ordinary mirror into a handsome piece of wall decor. Those who use it for a quick view of themselves will swear they never looked better!

DESIGNER: Diana Light

What You Need

Rectangular mirror (Hardware stores and glass wholesalers are great sources. The mirror in this project measures 28 by 11½ inches [72 x 29.5 cm].)

Simulated leading in liquid form

Crackle medium

Glass paint that simulates stained glass when dry, in royal blue and amber

Ruler

Black, water-based marker

What You Do

1. Wash and prepare the glass surface.

2. Based on the measurements of your mirror, use the ruler and marker to lightly mark a border of squares around the edges, with a rectangle at the center of the top and bottom border. In the project shown, the squares are 2 inches (5 cm) and the rectangles measure 3 by 4 inches (7.5 x 10 cm).

3. Add a diamond to the center of each rectangle.

4. Apply liquid leading along all the lines and around all four edges of the mirror. Let it dry.

5. Apply a thick layer of crackle medium directly from the bottle to every other square and to the diamonds.

6. Apply royal blue paint from the bottle to various squares, creating bands of crackle and blue squares along the longer edges of the mirror, using the project photo as a guide.

7. Once the first layer of crackle medium is dry, add a second layer.

8. Apply amber paint from the bottle to the edges around both diamonds and to the two outermost squares along the bottom of the mirror.

9. Let the paint cure at least seven days.

Watch Your P's and S's

These P's and S's prance all over a lively set of salt and pepper shakers. Simply jot yours in a pleasing jumble of styles and sizes to create tableware that springs to life.

DESIGNER: Kay Crane

What You Need

> Salt and pepper shakers
>
> Paints in black and white
>
> Small artist's brushes

What You Do

1. Wash and prepare the glass surfaces.

2. On one shaker, create freehand P's with white paint. On the other, create freehand S's with black. If you want more of a guide, copy letters from calligraphy books, magazines, newspapers, or fonts from a computer program to use as patterns, and transfer them to the glass first.

3. Use several coats of paint to get a bold, opaque look, letting the paint dry between coats.

4. Once the paint is thoroughly dry, bake it or glaze it according to the paint manufacturer's directions.

5. Paint a white ring around the screw-on top of the pepper shaker. Once the paint is dry, add black dots. Repeat the process, reversing the colors, on the salt shaker.

Tortoiseshell Vase

Deep, luxurious, layered colors transform a plain glass vase into a dazzlingly rich conversation piece.

DESIGNER: Colleen Webster

What You Need

> **Clear glass vase**
> **Glass paints in lemon yellow, caramel, antique brown, and black**
> **Artist's brushes (#8 and #6 flat)**

What You Do

1. Wash and prepare the glass surface.

2. Use the #8 brush to apply lemon yellow paint to the entire surface of the vase, leaving only the bottom free of color. Let the paint dry completely.

3. Load the #6 brush with caramel paint. Drag it in approximately 1-inch-long (2.5 cm) staggered strokes over the surface of the vase. Paint so that all your strokes run in the same direction. (In the project shown, the designer made her strokes at an angle, running in a circular fashion around the vase.) Cover the entire vase with these staggered strokes, leaving a visible background of yellow paint. Let the paint dry completely.

4. With a clean, dry #6 brush, use the same strokes described in step 3 to apply antique brown paint, this time staggering the strokes so that the brown overlaps the areas of yellow and caramel, creating a layered effect. Let the paint dry completely.

5. Again with a clean, dry #6 brush, add some black strokes to each layered patch to create contrast in the pattern. Let the paint dry completely.

6. If you wish, add additional strokes of any color to fine-tune the tortoiseshell look of your vase. You should end up with a light-to-dark layered look, with all of the colors showing through.

7. Once the paint is thoroughly dry, bake it or glaze it according to the paint manufacturer's directions.

Petroglyph Candle Lamp

*Primitive figures and symbols are the perfect thing to dance in
the flickering firelight of this frosty candle lamp.*

DESIGNER: Kay Crane

What You Need

Frosted glass candle lamp

Outliner in pewter, lead, or black

Carbon paper and pen

Patterns for this design appear on page 124. You can
also create your own, using illustrations from
books and magazines as a guide.

What You Do

1. Wash and prepare the glass surfaces.

2. Using carbon paper, transfer the figures you've
chosen to use to the shade and base of the lamp.

3. Fill in the transferred patterns with outliner,
squeezing it from the tube directly onto the glass surface. As you work, take pleasure in remembering that
the figures are meant to be crude, so precision isn't
the goal.

4. Create a simple border around the bottom of the
base. In the project shown, the designer piped a zigzag
border accented with dots.

Glass Fact

CRACKLE GLASS: Developed in
the 1500s in Venice, crackle
glass, created by dipping a
hot glass object into cold
water before reheating it,
looks like cracked ice.

Leopard-Print Clock

A few strategically placed patches of paint, and it becomes clear that this otherwise elegant clock has a bit of a wild side. Unleash your own with this easy technique.

DESIGNER: Colleen Webster

What You Need

> Clock with glass frame
>
> Glass paints in antique brown, black, lemon yellow, and caramel
>
> Artist's brushes (#6 flat and #1 round)
>
> Cotton swabs
>
> Palette or plastic lid for mixing paint

What You Do

1. Wash and prepare the glass surface.

2. Determine which side of the glass you will paint on (the front or the back), which will affect the sequence in which you apply the paint. For this project, the designer has painted on the back side of the glass, to create depth. If you want to paint on the front, apply the background first (step 6), then add the spots

3. Refer to figure 1 as a guide for painting the leopard spots. If you like, you can copy it and transfer it in a random fashion to your glass before painting.

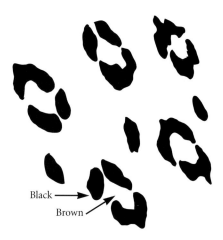

Figure 1

4. If possible, lay the clock flat for painting. Begin by applying the center marks in antique brown, using the round brush. This is the time to make adjustments in placement or shape. If you want to alter one of the marks, use a dampened cotton swab to remove any unwanted paint. Then reposition the mark. Let the brown marks dry completely.

5. Using a clean, dry round brush, apply black paint over the brown marks, using figure 1 as a guide for shape and placement. You may need to apply several coats of black paint to make it opaque. (The brown will still show through somewhat on the front of the

Glass Fact

The Fenton Art Glass Company, founded in Williamstown, West Virginia, in 1906, rose to prominence making carnival glass in the early 1900s and milk glass in the 1950s and '60s. It's one of the few early companies that survived the handmade glass slump of the 1940s and '50s.

clock. In step 7, you'll apply another coat of brown to accent the center markings.) Let the paint dry between coats, and allow it to dry completely when you're finished.

6. Mix approximately one part lemon yellow paint with two parts caramel to create a rich, amber color. With the flat brush, apply the amber paint evenly over the entire surface of the side you've been painting on. Allow the paint to dry, then apply a second coat if you want to deepen the amber color.

7. Using a clean, dry round brush fill in the center of each leopard print with antique brown. After it dries, you may want to add a second coat to deepen the tone, but don't allow the paint to become opaque.

8. Once the paint is thoroughly dry, glaze it according to the paint manufacturer's directions, if you wish.

Feather-Print Cocktail Glasses

Create a one-of-a-kind monogram from a sponged shape and a natural stamp, then use it to personalize an entire set of glasses before your next cocktail party.

DESIGNER: Katherine Duncan

What You Need

> Clear glass cocktail glasses
>
> Glass paints in periwinkle and brown
>
> Absorbent paper, such as craft paper or newspaper
>
> Palette or large plastic lid
>
> Several craft sponges in various shapes
>
> A handful of feathers (These can be purchased at a craft-supply store.)
>
> Artist's brush (½-inch [1.3 cm] flat)

What You Do

1. Wash and prepare the glass surfaces.

2. Assemble your materials on a surface covered in absorbent paper, and squeeze a circle of each color of paint onto the palette. Leave space around each of the colors.

3. Select one of the craft sponges for applying a base layer of paint (the designer used a triangular sponge first in the project shown). Press it into the periwinkle paint, and move it in circles until it absorbs the paint. Blot the excess paint from the sponge onto the absorbent paper until it prints with an opacity you like.

4. Press the sponge firmly into place in the center of one side of a glass. Remove it from the surface. If you haven't achieved a look you like, allow the paint to dry for a couple of minutes, add more paint to the sponge, and press over the first printing.

5. Turn the glass to the other side and print the same shape in the same manner. (Since you're working on clear glass, one shape will play off of the other as you look through the glass.)

6. Repeat this process on the other glasses in your set, and allow the paint to dry completely.

7. Select a feather and press it into the pool of brown paint on your palette. Once it has absorbed the paint, lay the feather on the paper and use the paintbrush to fan out its edges and distribute the paint evenly.

8. Try a test print or two on the same paper, adding more paint, if necessary, until you create an image you're happy with.

9. Clean and dry your brush, or have a new one on hand.

10. Lift the feather from the paper surface and hold it in front of one of the sponged shapes on a glass to determine its placement.

11. Lay the tip of the feather near the top of the glass and slowly, with the assistance of the clean artist's brush, press it in place over the sponged shape. Lift it off and repeat the process on the other side of the glass.

12. Repeat steps 7 through 11 on the other glasses in your set.

13. Once the paint is thoroughly dry, bake it or glaze it according to the paint manufacturer's directions.

Variation

Make each of the glasses in your set slightly different by using a variety of sponge shapes and/or different size feathers. You can also "print" some glasses with feathers only.

Glass Fact

MERCURY GLASS: This double-walled glass with a silver-colored lining (originally made of mercury) in between resembles actual silver. It became popular in the 19th century as an inexpensive substitute for the real thing in objects such as vases and candlesticks.

Dancing Tumblers

〜

Did someone say fun?! These plain old drinking glasses have gone playful, with jubilant little sprites romping atop mounds of multicolored dots.

DESIGNER: Margaret Desmond Dahm

What You Need

> **Set of tumblers**
> **Outliner (black)**
> **Glass paints in red, blue, and yellow**
> **Scissors**
> **Tape**
> **Small artist's brush (no larger than ⅛ inch [3 mm] wide)**
> **The patterns for this design appear on page 121.**

What You Do

1. Wash and prepare the glass surfaces.

2. Make two copies of each of the patterns of dancing figures on page 121. Cut out the figures and tape them (four total) on the inside of one of the glasses, so they're spaced evenly just below the rim.

3. Using the black outliner, draw the four figures on the front of the glass. Repeat the process on all the other glasses in your set.

4. Go back to the glass you started with. (Keep in mind that the outliner may not be completely dry. As you continue, hold each glass from the inside or at the base.) With the small brush, paint a row of red dots around the bottom, leaving enough space between the red dots to later add different-colored dots.

5. Add a second row of red dots above the first row, leaving even more space between the dots. Continue moving up the glass, lessening the dot density as you go. Paint only three or four dots on the row just beneath the feet of the figures. Repeat the process of painting red dots on all the other tumblers in your set.

6. With a clean, dry brush, fill in some of the area around the red dots on all of the glasses with blue dots. Again, the dot density should decrease as you work your way up the glass.

7. Add a set of yellow dots to all of the glasses, applying them with a clean, dry brush and following the same pattern.

8. Once the paint is thoroughly dry, bake it or glaze it according to the paint manufacturer's directions.

"Etched" Glass Decanter

White frost paint creates the subtle, elegant effect of finely etched glass—with none of the added effort. The look perfectly suits a handsome decanter like this one.

DESIGNER: Diana Light

What You Need

Clear glass decanter (Choose one with sharp
   angles, like the decanter in the project shown,
   if possible.)
White frost glass paint
Carbon paper and pen
Artist's brushes (round and fine liner)
Patterns for this design appear on page 122.

What You Do

1. Wash and prepare the glass surface.

2. With carbon paper, transfer the wave pattern on page 122, repeating it around the base of your decanter.

3. Transfer stars (including a shooting star, if you like) and a crescent moon (again, using the patterns on page 122) to the upper portion of the body of the decanter.

4. Using the round brush for the waves and the fine-liner brush for the stars and moon, paint the shapes with white frost paint.

5. White frost paint typically air dries, requiring no baking or glazing.

Earth-and-Sun Table

A daring design and rich, vivid colors transform a conventional table into a fabulous conversation piece. We provide you with everything you need to paint your own, from the pattern to the paint colors.

DESIGNER: Katherine Duncan

What You Need

Round glass tabletop (The tabletop shown measures 2 feet [60 cm] in diameter and ¼ inch [6 mm] thick.)

Table base with legs (The base shown is slightly smaller in diameter than the glass top. You should be able to find both tabletops and table bases at large home-supply stores.)

Absorbent paper

Bottle of squeezable glass paint in black

Glass paints in bright yellow, red, orange, dark green, medium green, light green, aqua, bright blue, shimmering blue, purple, silver, and black

Water-based black marker

Artist's brushes (½-inch [1.3 cm] flat and round)

Yellow and black felt pieces, each 2 feet (60 cm) square

Fabric glue

Scissors

The pattern for this design appears on page 121.

Photo 1

A note about the process: This table is "reverse" painted on the underside, meaning all of the final details are applied first and the background last. If you want to be able to flip the glass over and check your design on the front side as you work, leave a section of the glass unpainted on the edge.

What You Do

1. Wash and prepare the glass surface.

2. Use a photocopy machine to enlarge the pattern on page 121 to fit your table. (You may have to enlarge the pattern in sections, then piece them together.)

3. Cover your work surface with absorbent paper and place the enlarged pattern on top of it.

4. Place the glass tabletop on top of the pattern, lining up the edges of the design with the edges of the glass.

5. You can simply follow the pattern underneath as you paint or, for an added guide, outline the lines of the design first with the black marker.

6. Squeezing the black paint from its bottle, fill in the lines of the design. Let the paint dry.

7. Inside the outlines of the sun's rays and the circular band inside the rays, paint a small band of black paint with the ½-inch (1.3 cm) flat brush.

8. Before the paint dries, use the other end of the paintbrush to draw random, squiggly lines in the black paint, removing part of it and allowing the glass to show through. Let the paint dry.

9. Fill in the sun's outlines with areas of yellow, red, and orange. Paint over the black areas that you painted earlier, allowing the colors to shine through on the other side.

10. To paint the leaves, begin with random highlights of light green, then add medium green areas. Check your design from the front side as you work. Layer on aqua over some of the areas you've painted, then fill in remaining areas with the dark green.

11. For the waves, layer color as you did for the leaves, moving from the lightest to the darkest. Paint silver highlights along the edges of the waves first, add bright blue areas next, and finish with purple and black.

12. Use the squeezable black paint to outline the edge of the glass that you left blank at the beginning.

13. Once the paint is thoroughly dry, bake it or glaze it according to the paint manufacturer's directions.

14. Cut a semicircular pattern along one edge of the yellow felt. Trim the yellow felt to fit half of the table.

15. Cut the black felt into a circular piece that is slightly larger than the top of your table.

16. Use fabric glue to adhere the black felt to the tabletop, lapping the edges of the felt underneath the table. Place the yellow felt piece on top of the black one and glue it in place (see photo 1).

17. Paint the table legs with yellow glass paint (it works on wood too!).

18. Place the painted glass top on your table.

Confucian Bud Vase

Designer Kay Crane decided that kanji, the vertical Japanese writing system based on Chinese characters, beautifully suited this tall slender vase. The symbols she chose from the I Ching, *a part of the Confucian canon, represent "joy" and "nature"—a perfect combination for a vessel for flowers.*

DESIGNER: Kay Crane

What You Need

Bud vase

Gold glass paint

Scissors

Tape

Small artist's brush

Patterns for this design appear on page 121.

What You Do

1. Wash and prepare the glass surface.

2. Copy the patterns on page 121 (or choose others that you like). Cut the copied patterns out in a long strip. Insert it in the vase so that it shows through. Once you have the strip of paper in a straight position you're pleased with, tape it in place.

3. Paint the characters in gold, using several coats of paint, if necessary, to achieve the color you want.

4. Bake or glaze the vase, according to paint manufacturer's directions.

Black and White Plate Special

These striking studies in black and white, painted on the serving surfaces, make bold decorative dishware. The design can just as easily be painted on the back side of clear glass serving platters—or on an entire set of dinner plates.

DESIGNER: Nora C. Mosrie

What You Need

2 glass dinner plates (or more if you'd like to make a full dinner set)

Opaque glass paints in black and white

Artist's brush

Toothbrush (A sponge can be used as a substitute.)

What You Do

1. Wash and prepare the glass surfaces.

2. With the artist's brush, apply white paint to the outer rim of one plate and the center of the other. Let the paint dry completely.

3. Using a clean, dry artist's brush, apply black paint to the outer rim of the plate with the white center and to the center of the plate with the white rim. Let the paint dry completely.

4. With the toothbrush, blot paint on the rims of each plate (adding black paint to the white rim and white paint to the black rim), working toward a textured look. (If you are painting your plates on the back side, you would complete this step before adding the solid "background" layer of paint to the rim of each plate.)

5. Once the paint is thoroughly dry, bake it or glaze it according to the paint manufacturer's directions.

Modern Art Kitchen Canisters

Add deep, bold color and adventurous design to a formerly uninteresting corner of your kitchen. These easy, sponged canisters turn their spot by the stove into a mini art gallery.

DESIGNER: Katherine Duncan

What You Need

- Glass olive oil bottle (clean, labels removed)
- Two glass kitchen canisters with stoppers, one short and round and the other tall and rectangular
- Glass paints in brick red, olive green, yellow ochre, and brown
- Bottle of squeezable glass paint in black
- Palette or large plastic lid
- Artist's brush (1-inch [2.5 cm] flat)
- Several small, triangular craft sponges
- Paper towels
- Scrap of absorbent paper
- Sponge-tipped painting stick

What You Do

Olive Oil Bottle

1. Wash and prepare the glass surface.

2. Squeeze quarter-sized portions of brick red, olive green, and yellow ochre paint onto the palette or lid, leaving room around each color.

3. Load the artist's brush with brick red, and make a long, vertical stroke on each side of the bottle.

4. Allow the red strokes to dry for a few minutes. Then, with a clean, dry brush, layer overlapping strokes of yellow ochre at right angles on all four sides of the bottle. (You don't have to plan this! The design is meant to be free-form.) Let the paint dry.

5. Dip a sponge in the olive green paint, and blot the excess paint off on a paper towel. Test the sponge print on a piece of absorbent paper (keeping in mind that the paper will absorb the paint while the glass will not).

6. When you're satisfied with your test prints, begin dabbing the paint over the surface of the bottle with a random, back-and-forth motion. Be spontaneous, building your design as you go. If you make a mark you decide you can't live with, use a dampened paper towel to blot it off. Once you're satisfied with the look, let the paint dry.

7. On one side of the bottle, loosely "write" the word olive by squeezing the black paint over your layers of paint. (Again, don't worry about perfection! If you'd like, squeeze out a couple of test letters first on a piece of paper.)

8. Once the paint is thoroughly dry, bake it or glaze it according to the paint manufacturer's directions.

Round Pasta Jar

1. Wash and prepare the glass surface.

2. Dip a clean sponge into any one of the colors, blot the excess paint, then test some prints on the paper until you achieve the look you want.

3. Begin sponging triangular shapes in a wide band all the way around the center of the jar. (The prints don't have to look exactly like triangles. In fact, you can create interesting shapes by using an edge of the sponge or even dragging the sponge after pressing it on the glass. Experimentation is definitely allowed!) Let the paint dry.

4. Dip another clean sponge into a second color of paint and sponge a random motif on top of the first layer of color. You can create contrast by placing a lighter color over a darker one, or vice versa.

5. Repeat step 4, using the third color of paint.

6. Once the paint is thoroughly dry, bake it or glaze it according to the paint manufacturer's directions.

Tall Pasta Jar

1. Wash and prepare the glass surface.

2. Use a clean, dry artist's brush to lay a vertical strip of brick red on one half of one panel of the jar. Let the paint dry.

3. With a clean, dry brush, paint portions of the same panel (both red and clear areas) with yellow ochre. Paint over most of the red area, but leave some long rectangles of red visible. Likewise, paint over the clear area, but leave a couple of "windows" of unpainted areas so that the pasta (or whatever you put inside) will be semi visible. Let the paint dry.

4. Load the front of a clean sponge with olive green, and print random triangles on top of the second coat of paint.

5. Turn another sponge on its side, load the rectangular surface with brown, and add a couple of contrasting shapes to this section of the design.

6. Before the areas of sponged-on paint dry, use the end of your artist's brush to scribble over the surface, creating lines that allow the yellow ochre paint underneath to show through. Let the paint dry.

7. Use the black paint in the squeeze bottle to add free-form, curving lines on top of the painted areas and/or borders around the sponged-on shapes.

8. After you've applied all the paint, lay a sheet of paper towel over the top, press it, and remove much of the paint while blurring and melding the colors.

Sponge more colors of your choice on top of this paint while it's still wet, if you like.

9. It's up to you whether you paint only one panel of the jar, paint the two panels opposite each other, or cover all four panels in paint.

10. Once the paint is thoroughly dry, bake it or glaze it according to the paint manufacturer's directions.

Variation

On the tall pasta jar, omit step 8 (blotting with a paper towel) if you want a bolder look.

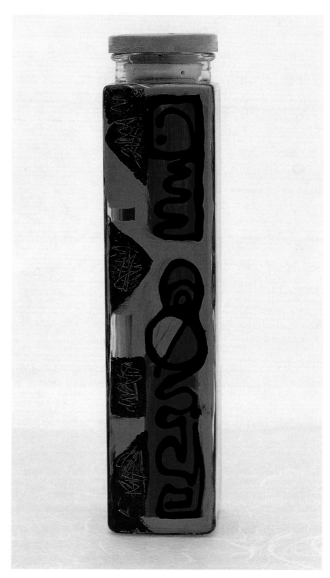

Island Party Platters

Dust off your grass skirt! Vibrant tropical colors transform plain glass platters in the shapes of fish into a reason for a luau.

DESIGNER: Heather Smith

What You Need

Clear glass fish-shaped platters featuring
    fish details
Shimmery glass paints in red, yellow-orange,
    purple, blue, teal, and light green
    (or other bright, tropical colors
    you find appealing)
Palette or plastic lids
Practice glass
Artist's brushes (small and medium)

What You Do

1. Wash and prepare the glass surfaces.

2. Select color combinations for each platter. For the project shown, the designer used red and yellow-orange for the small plate, purple and blue for the medium plate, and teal and light green for the large plate. On the palette or in the plastic lids, blend additional colors for each platter, so when you paint you can progress through various shades (dark to light) as you move from the outside of each platter in.

3. Paint the head and fins of each platter in a base color.

4. On each platter, dab paint into the scale depressions and the surrounding glass, working from the inner edge of the fins and head toward the center of the platter. Blend from darker to lighter shades as you work, making the transitions as smooth as possible.

5. Let the paint dry. You may decide to apply a second

coat of paint to the fins and heads to create a stronger, darker contrast with the centers of the platters.

6. Once the paint is thoroughly dry, bake it or glaze it according to the paint manufacturer's directions.

Tree of Life
Hurricane Lamp

A huge hurricane lamp (made for housing a burning candle) is the perfect stage for some primitive pageantry. Here, an exotic array of symbols, including a ceremonial mask, a flowing river, jungle birds, and a branching tree, come to life in the candlelight.

DESIGNER: Diana Light

What You Need

Large clear glass hurricane lamp

Translucent glass paints in violet, lemon yellow, orange, and scarlet

Simulated liquid leading

Matt varnish

Carbon paper and pen (optional)

Tape (optional)

Straight pin

Artist's brush (medium round)

Patterns for this design appear on page 124.

Glass Fact

JACK-IN-THE-PULPIT GLASS:
Glass vases shaped to resemble the Jack-in-the-pulpit flower date to the 1850s. They're still made today, primarily by Fenton Art Glass Company in Williamstown, West Virginia.

What You Do

1. Wash and prepare the glass surface.

2. Transfer the patterns on page 124 to the lamp by either taping them inside or using carbon paper and a pen to transfer them to the front. Place the sun mask in the upper center of the lamp, a bird on each side of the mask (one holding a fish), and the tree opposite the mask.

3. Use the straight pin to poke a tiny hole in the bottle of simulated leading (so it comes out in the thinnest stream possible).

4. Outline each of the figures. In addition, add a freehand river around the base of the lamp (including swirls of leading in the body of the river), three leaves at the end of each tree branch, and various large and small accent dots in open spaces (using the project photo as a guide). Let the outliner dry completely.

5. Paint the figures, using a clean, dry brush each time you switch to a new color and allowing each color to dry completely before you apply another next to it. Paint the sun mask orange, with violet accents on the head, eyes, mouth, and neck, and scarlet accents on the eyelids and lips. Paint the rays yellow. The bird bodies should be painted orange, with scarlet, yellow, and violet used to accent the eyes, wings, beaks, tails, and tufts of feathers on top of the heads. Paint various shades of "bark" on the tree, using yellow, orange, and scarlet. Fill in the river and leaves with violet, the fish with scarlet, orange, and yellow, and the larger dots with scarlet.

6. Once the paint is thoroughly dry, paint all remaining clear areas of the lamp with the matt varnish.

Tea Light Lanterns

*Everyone knows moths and light go together. Here's a
delightful way to pair them permanently on a charming
set of outdoor lanterns.*

DESIGNER: Diana Light

What You Need

Set of outdoor lanterns

Glass paints in chocolate, ivory, white, gold, silver, copper, and yellow

Paint pens in black, red, and yellow

Crackle medium

Outliner (gold)

Carbon paper and pen

Artist's brushes (fine liner)

Palette or plastic lid for mixing colors

Mineral spirits (optional; for removing mistakes made with solvent-based paint pens)

Patterns for this design appear on page 123. You can also come up with your own from drawings in books and photographs in magazines. Moth images in books and magazines can give you ideas for various markings and highlights, as well.

What You Do

1. Wash and prepare the glass surfaces.

2. Use carbon paper to transfer the patterns for moths and fireflies on page 123 to the glass panels on your lanterns. Place them in any arrangement you like—varying their placements on each panel.

3. Paint the figures with color combinations that appeal to you. Here are some suggestions, based on the designs shown.

Natural-Colored Moths

Paint a base coat of ivory on the wings. While the paint is still wet, use a mixture of chocolate and ivory to draw in a few simple vein lines. Paint a base coat on the moth bodies with the same mix of chocolate and ivory. Then, use chocolate paint for markings on the wings and a mixture of ivory and white for highlights on the wings. Add chocolate eyes, ivory antennae, chocolate and/or ivory markings on the bodies, and chocolate legs.

Metallic Moths

Use the gold outliner to outline the moth shapes, including eyes, antennae, bodies, wings, and a few simple interior lines. Add legs if you like, and let the outliner dry. Fill in the body with gold paint. Alternate silver and copper paint on the thorax and wings.

Fireflies

Draw in the figures you traced with the black paint pen, making a dot for the heads, two lines for the antennae, four lines for the wings, and a teardrop shape for the bodies. Once the black paint is dry, add a spot of red on each head. Fill in the bodies with yellow paint, and let the paint dry. Finally, apply crackle medium directly from the bottle, covering the glass panels and using the artist's brush to push the medium up next to each firefly shape.

4. Once the paint is thoroughly dry, bake it or glaze it according to the paint manufacturer's directions.

Stamped Glass Pins

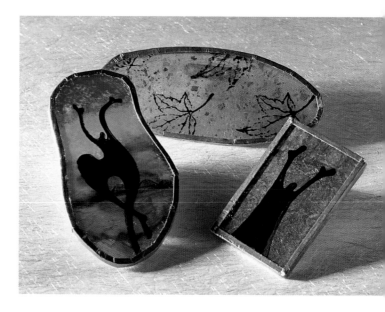

Shrink your focus, and a piece of painted glass becomes a miniature work of wearable art. These snazzy pins are a clever way to sharpen the look of any outfit.

DESIGNER: Lynn B. Krucke

What You Need

Small glass shape with a standard thickness of approximately 3/32 inch (.2 cm) (Although you can buy special tools to cut your own glass, that's an expense you may want to avoid if you plan to make only a few pins. A stained glass supply shop or a mirror and glass supplier should be able to cut glass into the shapes you want—and even grind the edges—for a minimal fee.)

Stamp (You will be creating a reverse image, so avoid stamps with writing on them.)

Permanent ink pad (black)

Glass paints in colors of your choice

Decorative paper or gift wrap

Pin backs (available at craft and beading stores)

Glue that dries clear

Copper foil tape (sold with stained glass supplies)

Sturdy craft glue for pin backs

Pencil

Scissors

Craft knife

Artist's brushes

What You Do

1. Wash and prepare the glass surface. (Wiping the glass piece with isopropyl alcohol helps the ink adhere.)

2. Ink your stamp with permanent ink and stamp its image on the glass. Avoid sliding or rocking the stamp, which could cause the image to blur. If you're stamping a solid image and it doesn't transfer completely, use a paintbrush to dab ink onto the places that need to be filled in. Let the stamped image dry completely.

3. If you'd like, paint the glass around the image in colors that suit your theme. Once the paint is thoroughly dry, bake it or glaze it according to the paint manufacturer's directions.

4. Thin the clear-drying glue slightly with water, brush an even coat of glue over the side of the glass you've been working on, and place the piece of decorative paper over the glass. Smooth the paper to press out any bubbles and let it dry.

5. Use the craft knife to trim the paper around the edges of the glass shape.

6. Apply copper foil tape to the edges of the piece to create a frame for the pin and finish the edges. Begin on one side and carefully smooth the tape around all of the edges. The tape should be centered on the edge of the glass. (Use a pencil or your fingernail to position it and smooth it around curves, as necessary.) Once you've wrapped tape around the entire piece, overlap the ends slightly.

7. Glue on the pin back with sturdy craft glue.

Variation

Since the stamped and painted side of your pin will be covered with paper, you can also add embellishments such as glitter, metallic leaf, or foil. Your added bit of ornamentation will show through to the front of the pin while remaining completely enclosed and protected.

Face Plates

Add a dash of abstract expressionism to your next dinner party. Your table will become its own art gallery with a dramatic set of plates like these.

DESIGNER: Susan Kinney

What You Need

Clear glass plates

Glass paints in black and white and bold colors like the orange, green, yellow blue, red, and turquoise in the plates shown

Outliner (black)

Selection of artist's brushes

Patterns for this design appear on page 122. You can also create your own, using illustrations from books and magazines as a guide.

What You Do

1. Wash and prepare the glass surfaces.

2. Copy the patterns on page 122 (or another that you've chosen), reducing or enlarging them so they fit the size of your plate.

3. Work on one plate at a time. Place the first plate upside down on top of one of the patterns.

4. Painting on the back of the plate and following the pattern underneath as a guide, use the black outliner to draw the face. Let the outliner dry.

5. Fill in the face, hair, background, and any other details with a mix of colors, using the plates shown as guides or creating your own combinations. You may want to mix paints to come up with out-of-the-ordinary shades. Unusual color choices, such as the green hair and two-toned yellow and purple face in the project shown on the left, give these plates their dramatic flair.

6. Repeat the process on the other plates in your set. You can use the same pattern for each plate, alternate it with the second pattern we've provided, or incorporate other patterns of your own.

7. Once the paint is thoroughly dry, bake it or glaze it according to the paint manufacturer's directions.

Seascape Water Bottle

Prop it in a prominent corner of a beach house and fill it with bright marbles—or sand and sea oats. Load it full of coins and make it a marine-theme piggy bank. Or, flip it over, hook it up, and you've got the snazziest water cooler around.

DESIGNER: Diana Light

What You Need

5-gallon water bottle

Stained glass spray paint in blue

Opaque glass paints in bright blue, yellow-orange, red-orange, and gold

Carbon paper and pen

Artist's brushes (both round and fine)

Patterns for this design appear on page 122.

Glass Fact

Glassware produced in northern Europe in the 16th and 17th centuries typically came from "forest glasshouses," glassworking settlements in deeply wooded countryside that was gradually cleared to fuel the roaring glass furnaces. Fittingly, the products of forest glasshouses had a characteristic greenish tint, but that had nothing to do with all the trees. It was caused by the iron that made the sand of northern Europe different from the sand in the south.

What You Do

1. Wash and prepare the glass surface.

2. Use carbon paper to transfer the fish pattern on page 122 to the bottle in a random fashion, positioning fish so that they swim back and forth. You may want to reduce and enlarge the pattern, so you have fish of various sizes. (If your bottle is ridged, keep the fish on the flat surfaces.) In addition, use the pattern on page 122 to transfer simple waves that flow in various directions.

3. Lightly fill in the wave patterns with the blue spray paint, leaving plenty of clear glass around them. Don't worry about staying within your pattern lines. The spray paint should creep beyond them so it creates a shadow effect once you paint over the wave patterns with bright blue. Let the paint dry.

4. With the round brush, paint the fish shapes in yellow-orange, red-orange, and gold. Let the paint dry.

5. On a few of the yellow-orange and gold fish, use the fine brush to add details (such as scales, eyes, and mouths) in red-orange. Let the paint dry.

6. With a clean, dry round brush, paint the wave patterns in bright blue, taking care not to cover all of the blue spray paint.

7. Add bright blue water bubbles of various sizes moving up the neck of the bottle.

Leapin' Lizards Chip & Dip Set

*Spoon in some salsa, surround it with mounds of
toasted tortilla chips, and let your guests uncover a
colorful collection of lizards crawling all over the
dish as they work their way down.*

DESIGNER: Diana Light

What You Need

Clear glass chip-and-dip-in-one dish

Opaque glass paints in blue, red-orange, pink, salmon, lavender, black, and white

Scissors

Tape

Water-based marker

Small artist's brushes (round and fine line)

Patterns for this design appear on page 123.

What You Do

1. Wash and prepare the glass surface.

2. Make multiple copies of the lizard pattern on page 123 (or copy others you like from books or magazines). Cut them out, tape them in a random arrangement on the outside of the bottom of the dish, lightly trace around them with the water-based marker, then remove the pattern pieces. You'll be left with the outline of lizard figures on the outside of your dish.

Note: You'll be reverse painting the lizards on the outside of the dish, meaning you'll add all of the foreground details first and the solid backgrounds last.

Glass Fact

MILK GLASS: This opaque, white glass resembling porcelain was first made in Venice during the 15th century. Its color comes from the tin oxide used to make it.

That way, when you look at the lizards through the dish, the foreground details appear to be painted on top of the background.

3. Begin by using a fine-line artist's brush to paint two small black dots for each lizard's eyes. Let them dry completely.

4. With a clean, dry fine-line brush, paint a white ring around each black dot to finish the eyes. Let the paint dry.

5. Outline each lizard in a solid color, using a clean, dry fine-line brush. Let the paint dry.

6. Use other colors and a fine-line brush to add patterns and details to each lizard, such as stripes, spots, and other markings, using the lizards on the project shown as a guide. Let the paint dry.

7. With the round brush, paint over each lizard in a color different from the colors you used for outlining and details.

8. Make several copies of the southwestern sun pattern on page 123. Tape three or four to the inside of the dish, just below the rim, anyplace you have large, unpainted spaces you want to fill.

9. Using the patterns as guides and clean, dry fine-line brushes, paint the suns. On each, paint the outer circle one color, the inside dot another color, and the rays a third color. Vary the color combinations for each sun. Remove the patterns.

10. Once the paint is thoroughly dry, bake it or glaze it according to the paint manufacturer's directions.

Fun-in-the-Sun Pitcher

This is a pitcher that plays, from the kids skipping rope along the flower-lined base to the dragonflies buzzing up the handle. Buy some primary paint colors and create your own tribute to summers full of free days.

DESIGNER: Diana Light

What You Need

Clear glass pitcher

Opaque glass paints in pine green, purple, red, bright blue, yellow-orange, and white

Water-based marker

Carbon paper and pen (optional)

Tape

Small, round artist's brush

Patterns for this design appear on page 122.

What You Do

1. Wash and prepare the glass surface.

2. If you'd like to follow a guide as you paint, transfer the patterns on page 122 to your pitcher. Make a copy of the sun and multiple copies of the flowers and dragonfly. Tape them to the inside of the pitcher, with the flowers in bunches around the base, the dragonflies toward the top, and the sun in the center of one side. Use carbon paper to transfer the dragonfly pattern and some creeping flowers up the handle if you're not comfortable adding these freehand.

3. Drawing on the front of the pitcher with a water-based marker, add words like those on the pitcher shown in a simple, child-like script. Finally, add some

simple figures and structures such as the children and lemonade stand shown here. Another way to add these images to your pitcher is to copy them from books or magazines, tape them inside the pitcher, and follow them as guides.

4. Begin filling in your patterns with paint. Paint the flower stems and grass patches green, the flower centers white, and the petals red. Mix and match colors for the dragonflies, painting the bodies and eyes one color and the wings another. Paint the sun yellow, and use a different solid color for each of the words. Paint your figures and structures in a variety of the colors listed.

5. Once the paint is thoroughly dry, bake it or glaze it according to the paint manufacturer's directions.

Faux Stained Glass Window

The old-world elegance of stained glass isn't out of reach for those of us who lack the time and know-how to connect fragments of colored glass with soldered-together lead. Here's an easy way to achieve a strikingly similar look. The designer created her playful version on an old windowpane and equipped it with a chain for hanging.

DESIGNER: Mona-Katri Makela

What You Need

Windowpane (Check flea markets and renovation supply stores.)

Simulated leading in liquid form (For the project shown, with a glass surface of 14 by 28 inches [35 x 72 cm], the designer used two large bottles of liquid leading.)

Glass paint that simulates stained glass when dry in kelly green, emerald green, cocoa brown, white, ivory, ruby red, and blue

Small nail

Scissors or craft knife

Cotton swabs

Combing tool such as a toothpick

Straight pin

2 screw hooks

Chain

The pattern for this design appears on page 123.

What You Do

1. Use a photocopy machine to enlarge the pattern on page 123 to fit your windowpane.

2. Place the pattern on your work surface and lay the window (with the side that is to be the finished front facing up) on top of it.

3. Use the small nail to poke a hole in the tip of the bottle of simulated leading, and shake the leading into the tip. Outline the design on the front of the window, squeezing leading from the bottle straight onto the glass, as if you were piping icing. In addition, run a border of leading all the way around the edge where the glass meets the window's frame.

4. Let the leading dry completely (at least four hours). Once it's dry, you can trim any overlaps of leading strips with scissors or a craft knife and press the trimmed strips back in place.

5. The dried leading provides raised outlines for each of the sections you'll color in with paint. Following the color notes on the pattern on page 123,

begin applying one color at a time. You'll use kelly green for the frog's body and for some of the leaves, ivory for the frog's markings, emerald green for the other leaves, cocoa brown for the brown sections of the branch, cocoa brown mixed with ruby red for the other sections of the branch (apply the red on top of the brown while the brown is still wet), ruby red for the accents on the water plants, blue for the water, and white for the ripples in the water. To apply the paint, squeeze out thin lines from the bottle straight onto the glass, moving the bottle tip back and forth as you work and completing an entire section before stopping. Make sure you paint all the way up to the leading. Use cotton swabs to remove wet paint from the leading or from the window frame.

6. After completing a section, use a toothpick or a similar tool to "comb" through the paint and even it out, if necessary. Use the straight pin to pop any bubbles.

7. Once the paint is completely dry (refer to the manufacturer's notes), you may want to use simulated leading to outline the design on the other side of the window, giving it a more finished look.

8. If you want to hang your finished piece, add two screw hooks to the top of the frame, and connect them to a chain.

Glass Fact

In baseball, a pitcher who has a particularly sore or weak arm is said to have a glass arm. Boxers often describe vulnerable body areas as being made of glass; thus, they occasionally experience glass jaws, glass heads, and glass guts.

Decorative Fireplace Screen

Weathered window sashes, beaded wire, and glass paints aren't the typical ingredients that come to mind when you think of crafting your own fireplace screen. And they're just what make this clever take on an otherwise ordinary home fixture such fun!

DESIGNER: Kim Ballor

What You Need

2 old window sashes (The sashes in the project shown are 24 inches [60 cm] square.)

Simulated leading in liquid form

Glass paint that simulates stained glass when dry, in turquoise, kelly green, lime green, denim blue, amethyst, magenta, and aqua

18-gauge craft wire in magenta and aqua

About 12 dozen assorted glass beads

Small nail

Scissors or a craft knife

Cotton swabs

Straight pin

2 hinges with screws

Screwdriver

Craft drill

Wire cutters

Needle-nose pliers

The pattern for this design appears on page 122.

Glass Fact

GLASS CEILING: Something you might hit on the way up if your company has a history of failing to promote people like you (your gender, race, etc.) beyond a certain level.

What You Do

1. Increase the dragonfly pattern on page 122 to a size that fits your windows. You may want to also copy just parts of the dragonfly (wings and the tail, for example) to place on the edges (refer to the project photo as a guide).

2. Place the pattern(s) on your work surface, and lay one of the windows (with the side that is to be the finished front facing up) on top of it.

3. Use the small nail to poke a hole in the tip of the bottle of simulated leading, shake the leading into the tip, and lead all the lines of the pattern.

4. Add free-form background lines of leading running diagonally. (Again, refer to the project photo as a guide.)

5. Rearrange the pattern pieces a bit, and lead the pattern lines and free-form background lines on the second window. Let the leading dry on both windows for at least four hours. Once it's dry, you can trim any overlaps of leading strips with scissors or a craft knife and press the trimmed strips back in place.

6. Paint the dragonflies using lime green, kelly green, and turquoise, altering the placement of the three colors on each dragonfly. The dried leading provides raised outlines for each of the sections you'll color in with paint. To apply the paint, squeeze out thin lines from the bottle straight onto the glass, moving the bottle tip back and forth as you work, filling in each section solidly. Make sure you paint all the way up to

the leading. Use cotton swabs to remove wet paint from the leading or from the window frame. After finishing a section, pop any large air bubbles with a straight pin.

7. Paint the background sections, alternating the remaining paint colors. Simply "scribble" the paint from the bottle in this case, without filling in the sections solidly. Let the paint dry completely, until it is transparent.

8. Screw the hinges to the inside edges of each window frame to connect the two as a screen. Position one about 2 inches (5 cm) below the tops of the frames and the other about 2 inches (5 cm) above the bottoms.

9. Use needle-nose pliers, a random collection of beads, and the magenta wire to create short sections of beads and twisted wire, each measuring approximately 1½ to 2 inches (3.8 to 5 cm). Use the suggested arrangements in figure 1 as guides. Create enough sections so that, once they are connected into a strand, they easily drape from one end of a window sash to another. Connect each section in the strand by twisting tiny round circles of wire "jump" rings (see figure 2).

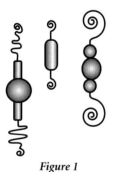

Figure 1

Figure 2

10. Create another strand of beaded wire sections with the magenta wire, then create two similar strands using aqua wire. Make the aqua strands slightly longer than the magenta strands.

Beaded fringe

11. Hook one magenta strand and one aqua strand together at the ends, then do the same with the other two strands.

12. At the ends of each two-part strand, twist on 3-inch (7.5 cm) tails of wire.

13. Using the craft drill, drill small holes on the top ends of each window.

14. Slide the wire tails into each hole to attach the beaded strands.

15. If you like, twist short sections of beaded wire fringe onto the outer edges of each hanging strand.

Detail of wing

Picnic Casserole Dish

This dish's red-and-white-checked pattern is covered with—what else— stamped-on ants. Fill it with your favorite casserole and you've got a complete picnic in a pan.

DESIGNER: Lynn B. Krucke

What You Need

- Square casserole dish
- Painter's tape or masking tape
- Glass paints in red and white or ivory
- Permanent ink pad with black ink
- Ant stamp
- Pencil
- Artist's brushes (½ inch [1.3 cm] flat and 1 inch [2.5 cm] flat)
- Ruler

What You Do

1. Wash and prepare the glass surface.

2. Place a strip of tape, firmly pressed in place, around the top of the dish.

3. Turn the dish upside down. Using white or ivory paint and the larger brush, paint the un-taped outside surface of the dish, covering the sides and the bottom. Let it dry, then add a second coat for a more opaque finish. Let the paint dry completely.

4. Use the ruler and pencil to mark the tape (still in place along the top edge of the dish) at ½-inch (1.3 cm) intervals all the way around the dish. These marks will be your guides for the first row of red squares.

5. With the ½-inch (1.3 cm) brush and red paint, begin at one corner of the dish and paint a ½-inch (1.3 cm) square. Since the brush is the width of the square you want to paint, this is a one-stroke process: load it with paint, press it onto the dish at the edge of the tape, pull it down until the square is as long as it is wide, then lift the brush. Continue around the dish.

6. After the first row, drop down to create a second row. This time, paint the squares between those on the first row. When you're finished, add a third row, alternating the squares again. Continue with more rows until you reach the bottom of your dish. Let the paint dry.

7. Ink the ant stamp with permanent ink, and stamp ants randomly around on the dish. Work fairly quickly; permanent ink is fast to dry.

8. Remove the tape and bake or glaze the dish according to the paint manufacturer's directions.

Aquarium Block

Glass blocks (which you can find at home- and-building supply stores) have become high-end interior design elements, showing up as everything from bookends and paperweights to the building blocks for shower walls. Here's a clever way to capture an aquatic scene in one of yours.

DESIGNER: Betty Auth

What You Need

- Square glass building block
- Glass paints in tangerine, watermelon, cantaloupe, white, dark and light blue, yellow green, olive, dark hunter green, and black
- Sponge
- Artist's brushes (flat and round, small)
- Scissors
- Pencil or black water-based marker
- Paper towels
- Palette or plastic lids
- Painter's tape or masking tape
- A pattern for the fish appears on page 122.

What You Do

Most of this design is "reverse" painted on the back side of the block, meaning you'll begin with each image's top layer (the eyes on a fish, for example) and work your way through the background layers (the fins, the body, and the background water).

1. Wash and prepare the glass surfaces (on both the front and the back of the block).

2. Lay the block flat and run a line of tape along each edge, forming a frame around the flat surface.

3. Make multiple copies of the fish pattern on page 122 (varying the size from copy to copy, if you'd like).

4. Cut out the fish shapes and arrange them on the flat surface until you're happy with the design, then trace around each shape lightly with the pencil or marker. Remove the patterns.

5. Dip the very tip of one of your brush handles into black paint and make a dot for an eye on each fish.

6. Use the round brush to paint simple stripes or wavy lines on each fish, using bright colors. Let the paint dry.

7. With the flat brush, fill in the fish bodies, tails, and fins with tangerine.

8. Make small white circles for bubbles coming up from the fish to near the masking tape around the top of the glass. Let the paint dry.

Glass Fact

Admiring what she believed to be a shimmering pool of water in the courtyard of King Solomon's ninth-century palace, the Queen of Sheba lifted her skirts to cross it. She soon learned that she had revealed her royal limbs for naught—the courtyard floor was actually made of glass.

9. Add shadows around the bubbles with dark blue, and let the paint dry.

10. Moisten the sponge, squeeze out any excess water, dip it in light blue, and use it to coat the entire background, painting right over the fish. (You may want to mix some white paint with your light blue to achieve a background color you're happy with.) Allow the paint to dry, and remove the tape.

11. Turn the block over to the front side, and place a strip of tape along the bottom of the block.

12. Paint some curving stalks of sea grass rising up from the masking tape to about halfway up the block. Alternate among the various colors of green from stalk to stalk. Be careful not to add so much grass that it covers the fish. Allow the paint to dry, and remove the masking tape.

13. Once the paint is thoroughly dry, bake it or glaze it according to the paint manufacturer's directions.

Ladies Only

Want to be sure your painted glass piece will be noticed? Have we got the project for you! (This is also the perfect undertaking for anyone into the trend of salvaging and sprucing up cast-off architectural elements.) Designer Dana Irwin used a Matisse-inspired design and a vintage sign to transform an old door into a new conversation piece. You can do the same by copying her easy-to-follow pattern to a glass-paned door of your own. Use your finished piece as a functional door, suspend it from the ceiling as a work of art, or cover it with a sheet of glass and turn it into a one-of-a-kind table.

DESIGNER: Dana Irwin

What You Need

Door with glass panel (Antique shops, flea markets, and renovator supply stores are the best sources.)

Practice glass

Glass paints in white, ochre, sky blue, aqua, pink, and peach (You may want to add a bit of white to the peach to make it more flesh toned.)

Simulated leading in liquid form

Clear acrylic spray gloss (optional)

Tape

Small nail

Scissors or a craft knife

Selection of artist's brushes (You'll want larger, flatter brushes for the body areas and smaller, rounded brushes for the highlights.)

The pattern for this design appears on page 121.

What You Do

1. Wash and prepare the glass surface.

2. Use a photocopy machine to enlarge the pattern on page 121 to fit the glass panel on your door. (You may have to enlarge the pattern in sections, then piece them together.)

3. Tape the pattern to the glass on what will be the front of your door, so it shows through to the back. You'll apply the paint to the glass on the back side of the door.

4. Use the small nail to poke a hole in the tip of the bottle of simulated leading and shake the leading into the tip. Outline the design, using the pattern as a guide. Squeeze the leading from the bottle straight onto the glass, as if you were piping icing.

5. Let the leading dry completely (at least four hours). Once it's dry, you can trim any overlaps of leading strips with scissors or a craft knife and press the trimmed strips back in place.

6. The dried leading provides raised outlines for each of the sections you'll color in with paint. Paint in an abstract, sketchy fashion, using the project photo as a guide. Let each color dry before you move on to the next, and use a clean, dry brush each time you switch colors. Start by painting half of the face with peach, leaving a bit of clear glass where the figure's eye would be. Continue by filling in most of the chest and arm areas in peach. Outline the edges of the legs in peach as well. Blend in ochre accents along the edges of the chest and arm areas. With sky blue, streak the side and bottom of the chair. Add streaks of aqua to the side of the chair, and paint some blotchy aqua dots below the sky-blue streaks on the bottom of the chair. Use pink to paint a smudge of blush on the unpainted side of the figure's face. Finally, add white, shadow-like highlights on the curves of the legs, above the blushed cheek, and on the arms, chest, and stomach areas.

7. When all of the paint is completely dry, spray clear, acrylic gloss evenly over the entire painted area, if you like. Be sure to try this on a piece of practice glass first. The gloss may dull the "glassy" character of the piece more than you want it to. If so, skip this step.

Glass Fact

Glassmaking was North America's first industrial enterprise, begun in 1608, when eight German and Polish glassmakers, members of Captain John Smith's first group of colonists, built a glass furnace and set to work.

Gallery

The following pages showcase the work of contemporary artists who specialize in painting on glass. Their pieces feature a variety of styles, as well as numerous techniques and materials which are beyond the scope of those outlined in this book. We include them as a source of inspiration—and as outstanding examples of the range of possibilities for combining paint and glass.

Above: WD40+ (WALT LIEBERMAN AND DICK WEISS); *Boy with Tulips*, 1997; 21" x 24" (54 x 61.5 cm); fired enamel on glass. Photo: Roger Schreiber

Left: MARY B. WHITE; *Voyages*, 1992; 11" x 13" (27.5 x 32.5 cm); reverse painting on blown, etched glass. Photo: Doug Keister

Above: JUDY JENSEN; *Mixed Deck*, 1997; 20" x 34½" (50 x 88.5 cm); reverse painting on glass with oil pastel, wax oil, colored pencil, acrylic paint, spray enamel, spray lacquer, gold leaf, glitter. Photo: Emil Vogely

Right: JOHN DE WIT; *Horse Latitudes*, 1999; 27½" x 11" (70.5 x 27.5 cm); blown and painted glass. Photo: Rick Semple

Far right: JOHN DE WIT; *Symbols*, 1997; 26" x 12 " (66.5 x 30.5 cm); blown and painted glass. Photo: Rick Semple

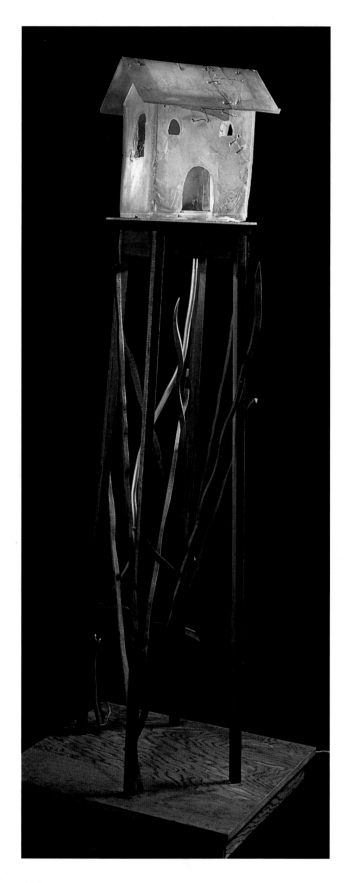

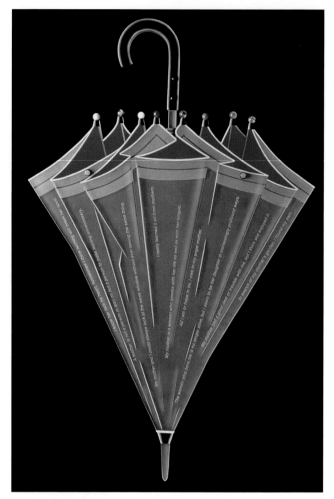

Above: SUSIE KRASNICAN; *Rain or Shine*, 1998; 35¼" x 22" x ½" (90.5 x 56.5 x 1.5 cm); enamel on sandblasted glass. Photo: Mark Gulezian

Writing on umbrella: I know her face by heart. Sometimes I think nothing will break her spell. A mother is not a person to lean on but a person to make leaning unnecessary. My mother and I could always look at the same window without ever seeing the same thing. I really learned it all from mothers. My mother is a person who speaks with her life as well as with her tongue. All I am or hope to be I owe to my angel mother. The woman who bore me is no longer alive, but I seem to be her daughter in increasingly profound ways. My mother had a great deal of trouble with me, but I think she enjoyed it. In search of my mother's garden, I found my own.

Above left: MARY B. WHITE; *Fall Dwelling*, 1995; 50" x 13" (128 x 32.5 cm); recycled steel, reverse-painted glass. Photo: Doug Keister

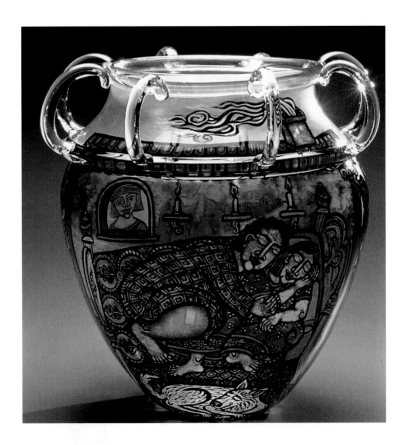

Above: CAPPY THOMPSON; *Lovers Dreaming a Dream*, 1996; 16" x 16" x 16" (40 x 40 x 40 cm); reverse painting with vitreous enamels on blown glass. Photo: Michael Seide

Above right: CAPPY THOMPSON; *Searching for the Bodhisattva: A Spirit Canoe Carries My Soul toward the Divine Child of My Dreams,* 1996; 21" x 11½" x 11½" (54 x 29.5 x 29.5 cm); reverse painting with vitreous enamels on blown glass. Photo: Michael Seide

Right: CASEY PHILLIPS; *Mermaid*, 1994; 18" x 24" (45 x 62 cm); painted and fired glass, marbles, foil, solder, zinc. Photo: Casey Phillips

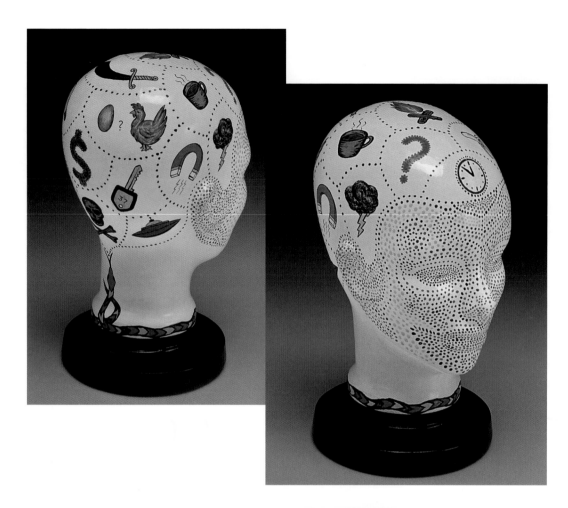

Above: RICK MELBY;
Head Games, 1999; 12" x 6" x 8" (30 x 15 x 20 cm); blown glass, thermohardening glass paints, wood. Photo: Tim Barnwell

Left: JUDY JENSEN;
Dervishes, 1996; 28" x 33½" (72 x 86 cm); reverse painting on glass with oil pastel, wax oil, colored pencil, acrylic paint, spray enamel, spray lacquer, gold leaf, glitter.
Photo: Emil Vogely

Above: ROBERT CARLSON; *Ramas'*
Pavillion, 1987; 10" x 34" (25.5 x 87 cm);
enamel on blown glass. Photo: Robin Stancliff

Above right: MARY LYNN WHITE;
Alpine Landscape, 1996; 10" x 7" (25 x 17.5
cm); glass enamel paint, furnace-blown
vessel. Photo: John Littleton

Right: HENRY HALEM; *Czech Vessel,*
1997; 24" x 10" x 11" (62 x 25 x 27.5 cm);
reverse painting on glass with wax pencil,
precious leaf. Photo: Henry Halem

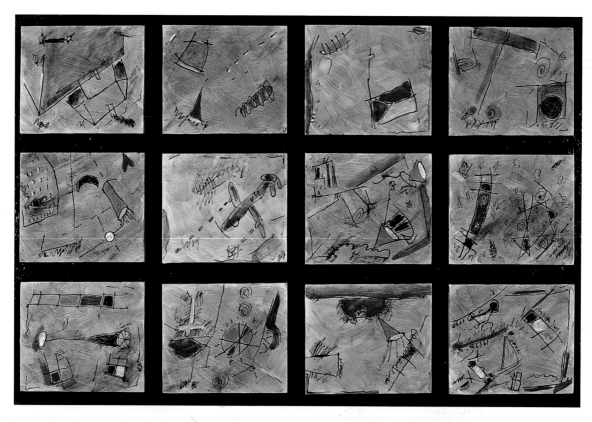

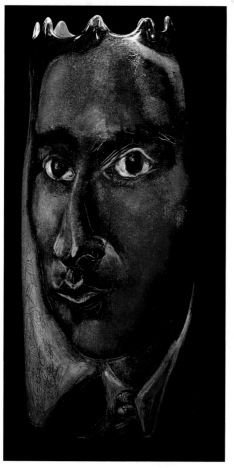

Above: HENRY HALEM; *Biograph II*, 1993; 17" x 25" x 3" (43.5 x 64 x 8 cm); fired glass enamels on vitro-lite. Photo: Henry Halem

Bottom left: WD40+ (WALT LIEBERMAN AND DICK WEISS); *Our Soldier Our Father*, 1994; 23" (59 cm); fired enamel on glass. Photo: Roger Schreiber

Bottom right: KATE DWYER; *Emil*, 1998; 12" x 24" (30 x 62 cm); reverse painting. Photo: Myron Galger

Patterns

Reduce or enlarge to fit your piece of glass

Alpine Hot Chocolate Mugs
Page 56

Bowl of Flowers
and Dots
Page 54

Colored Bottle Set
Page 31

Confusion
Bud Vase
Page 86

Dancing Tumblers
Page 82

Hanging Vase
Page 53

Earth-and-Sun Table
Page 84

Ladies Only
Page 112

Face Plates
Page 97

Decorative Fireplace Screen
Page 106

Fun-in-the-Sun Pitcher
Page 102

"Etched" Glass Decanter
Page 83
Waves for Seascape Water Bottle
page 98

Fluted Platter
Page 50

Seascape Water Bottle
page 98
Aquarium Block
page 110

Spring Table Set
Page 42

Morning Glory Plate
Page 58

A= kelly green

B=emerald green

C=cocoa brown

D=white

E=ivory

F=ruby red

All blank sections should be painted blue

Faux Stained Glass Window
Page 104

Powder Room Set
Page 40
Floral Doorknobs
page 46

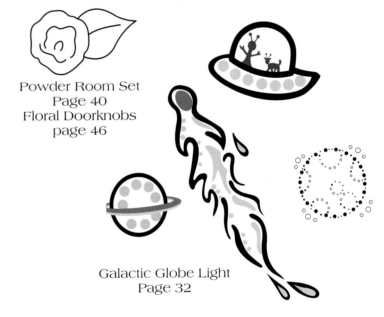

Galactic Globe Light
Page 32

Garden Party Lights
Page 52

Tea Light Laterns
Page 94

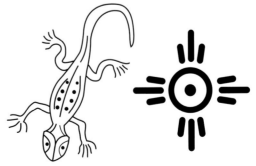

Leapin' Lizards Chip & Dip Set
Page 100

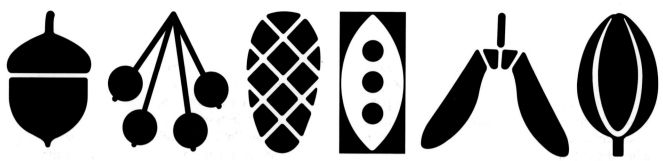

Painted Window Room Divider
Page 44

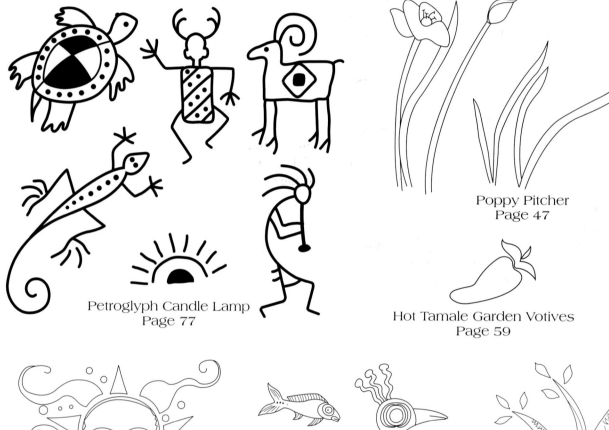

Poppy Pitcher
Page 47

Petroglyph Candle Lamp
Page 77

Hot Tamale Garden Votives
Page 59

Tree of Life Hurricane Lamp
Page 92

Contributing Designers

Betty Auth is a free-lance designer, author, and editor who writes a regular column for *Krause's Arts Magazine* and contributes to many other craft and design publications. Her main areas of design interest include woodburning, colored pencil work, crazy quilting and embellishment, and other creative mediums.

Kim Ballor has been a designer in the craft industry for 15 years. She has had numerous articles published in magazines, authored 16 how-to books, and has taught the world to craft through television programs, videos, and workshops.

Amy Cook devotes the bulk of her time to creating, producing, selling, reading, and imagining books. Supplemental passions include education, fine art, and that favorite Asheville, North Carolina, pastime, hiking. Fellow Appalachian State University graduate **Les Caison III** keeps his budding painting career afloat however he can.

Kathy Cooper is a full-time floorcloth artist producing original handpainted floorcloths in custom designs for clients, designers, and selected galleries. Cooper's paintings depict two-dimensional, sometimes whimsical graphic images in rich, wonderful colors. Her images come from her personal experiences, the garden, her kids, and all of the visual stimulation around her. Kathy Cooper Floorcloths, Route 5, Box 214, King, North Carolina 27021. Website: www.kathycooperfloorcloths.com

Kay Crane is primarily an animal and wildlife artist whose love of nature recently brought her to Colorado to live. Her work has appeared in shows and galleries around the world, but her greatest pleasure comes from drawing and painting animals, whether it be pet portraits or animals in the wild, and it is to this that she always returns. Kay lives with her husband, Kim, and their small dog, Blitz. She welcomes inquiries and correspondence regarding her work: kandk@gjct.net

Margaret Desmond Dahm lives in Asheville, North Carolina, where she runs a typesetting business with her husband and hand prints silk screen designs.

Katherine Duncan currently spends her days working as an editor and author for Lark Books in Asheville, North Carolina, and somehow finds time to create fabulous projects on the side! Prior to her present occupation, Katherine worked for many years as a museum curator and director. She has had a lifelong interest in writing and the arts.

Dana Irwin is an artist who works in many different media. Her artwork has appeared in many nationally distributed books and magazines. She lives in Asheville, North Carolina, with her two dogs, two cats, and her accordion in a very tolerant neighborhood.

Susan Kinney is a designer specializing in eclectic interiors, glass and clay jewelry, fabric and rug design, and computer-generated artwork. She attributes the Oriental influence in many of her designs to her years living in Japan and Hawaii. She can be reached at her interior design business, Suezen Designs, in Asheville, North Carolina, at suezendesigns@home.com.

Megan Kirby is a weekend crafter currently living in Asheville, North Carolina.

Lynn B. Krucke lives in Summerville, South Carolina, with her husband and daughter. She has long been fascinated with handcrafts of all types, and her favorite projects incorporate elements from more than one craft.

Diana Light, currently residing in Asheville, North Carolina, is an accomplished artisan specializing in painted glass. Her delicate images and vibrant colors combine with the translucent properties of glass to create unique objects for everyday use. More of her work can be viewed at www.eden.rutgers.edu/~upchurch.

Laurey-Faye Long is an all-around crafter from Marshall, North Carolina, where she lives with her husband, woodworker Steve Tengelsen, and a host of four-legged creatures ranging from cat and hounddog to the goat and sheep they recently acquired to help mow the grass.

Contributing Designers

Shelley Lowell is an award-winning graphic designer, illustrator, and fine artist. Her paintings and sculpture have been exhibited in museums and galleries in many cities throughout the United States. She resides in Alexandria, Virginia, with her two cats.

Mona-Katri Makela was a student at the Rudolph Steiner School in Helsinki, Finland, from kindergarten on. The experience provided her with an appreciation for art and expression. In addition to glass painting, she does various other forms of art and design work.

Kelly McMullen is a graphic designer and artist currently living in Durham, North Carolina. She makes functional ceramic art, handmade paper lamps, and handpainted furniture.

Nora C. Mosrie works in various media to create original paintings, drawings, fabric designs, and embellished surfaces. Her paintings and drawings have been exhibited in both solo and group shows throughout the mid-Atlantic and southeastern states.

Casey Phillips, an award-winning glass artist, works primarily with kiln-fired glass paints, creating one-of-a-kind pieces for galleries, arts shows, and individuals.

Sally Rhett earned a BFA from Converse College in Spartanburg, South Carolina, where she studied painting, photography, pottery, metal sculpture, and horticulture. Her artwork is an interpretation of her respect for and awe of nature. For a color catalog of her work, contact her at: sallymanders@worldnet.att.net.

Heather Smith, assistant editor at Lark Books, grew up on the coast of Maine, where she occasionally returns to teach environmental education to children. Now that she's relocated to western North Carolina, she enjoys hiking, mountain biking, and, of course, crafting in her cozy home in Asheville.

Katheryn M. Smolski grew up surrounded by the handicrafts and artwork of her native Asheville, North Carolina, where she spent much of her time creating original pieces as gifts for family and friends. Inspired by floral and geometric influences imbued with a touch of whimsy, she recently began producing her own unique designs for painted glass with an emphasis on stemware and votive candle holders. Currently Katheryn lives with her husband in New Jersey and continues to develop new works of art for practical use. You can reach her at 973-568-3198 or Katheryn@cigarboy.com.

Dorris Sorensen has enjoyed every facet of the decorative painting industry. She started as a student, then turned teacher, shop owner, professional crafter, designer, author, and television personality. Dorris has written more than 36 books, numerous magazine articles, and various advertisements, and is a proud member of the Delta Design Force and of the Society of Craft Designers.

Tracy Page Stilwell creates dolls, quilts, painted furniture, and mixed-media projects. She is also known as a teacher, student, and curator, and can often be found in the garden.

Travis Waldron resides in the mountains surrounding Asheville, North Carolina, where she creates quilted works, clothing designs, gourd vessels, painted glass objects, nautical knot works, and jewelry from found objects. She also has a private practice as a feminist therapist, where she seeks to encourage folks to approach life challenges with a true sense of creativity.

Colleen Webster studied fine art in New York City. She currently lives and works in Asheville, North Carolina. Feeling driven to produce and create, her work touches upon the beauty of color and technique.

Billie Worrell lives in Columbia, Tennessee. She has been a member of the Delta Design Force since 1992, has taught product training seminars and workshops across the country, and has published numerous articles about her work.

Gallery Artists

Robert Carlson is an award-winning glass artist who has exhibited extensively in the United States and Europe. He lives and works in Washington.

John de Wit is a glass artist who lives and works in the Pacific Northwest. He began glassworking at California State University in Chico in 1976. Subsequently, he has worked for Orient and Flume Art Glass and Dale Chihuly. Since 1989, John has been producing his own artwork, which is shown in select galleries throughout the United States and Europe.

Kate Dwyer creates her reverse paintings in a rural studio near Asheville, North Carolina. She is represented by several galleries in the United States.

Henry Halem is a studio artist producing architectural commissions as well as individual objects.

Judy Jensen is a glass painter from Austin, Texas, who has exhibited extensively in addition to teaching workshops and classes on reverse painting techniques.

Susie Krasnican lives and works outside of Washington, D.C.

Walter Leiberman is a Seattle-based glass artist.

Rick Melby creates one-of-a-kind lamps and sculpture from a variety of media. He has exhibited and been collected internationally.

Casey Phillips, an award-winning glass artist, creates one-of-a-kind and limited-edition pieces for individuals and businesses throughout the United States.

Seattle artist **Cappy Thompson** is internationally known for her reverse-painted narrative vessels shown at Leo Kaplan Modern in New York City.

Dick Weiss lives and works in Seattle, Washington.

Mary B. White started working with glass as a glassblower, but reverse glass painting has been part of her expression since 1980, when she created a series of reverse glass paintings for her MFA exhibition. Her current artistic investigation also includes building and casting a series of glass houses on a variety of scrap wood and steel foundations. Many of the houses are painted.

Mary Lynn White shares a studio with her husband, Gary Beecham, where they create painted and canework vessels, sculptural forms, and fused-glass jewelry.

Acknowledgments

Much Thanks …

To Angela Scherz and Pebeo for providing many of our designers with the glass paints they used to create their projects.

To Robert Chiarito of Penland School of Crafts, Ruth Summers of the Southern Highland Craft Guild, and designer Betty Auth, who were most generous with their time (and address books). They helped steer us toward many of the talented project designers and gallery artists featured in this book.

To The Natural Home and Complements to the Chef, both in Asheville, North Carolina, for allowing us to pick and choose photo-shoot props from their fabulous stores. Visit the Complements to the Chef website at www.complementstothechef.com.

To Biltmore Estate, Asheville, North Carolina, for lending the image that appears on page 9 (bottom); Mint Museum of Art, Charlotte, North Carolina, for lending the image that appears on page 8; and The Corning Museum of Glass, Corning, New York, for lending the images that appear on pages 7 and 9 (top).

And thank you, *thank you* to designer Diana Light, who not only created many splendid projects featured in this book, but also painted the samples scattered throughout the Basics section and devoted days (and much rigor!) to testing paints and techniques, then contributed her resulting expertise. Her talent, imagination, integrity, playful spirit, and love of the art of painting on glass shine through on many of this book's pages.

Index